The Story of
Acadia
National Park

The Complete Memoir of the Man
Who Made It All Possible

GEORGE B. DORR
The "Father of Acadia"

ACADIA PUBLISHING COMPANY
Bar Harbor, Maine

ISBN 0-934745-21-8

PUBLISHER'S NOTE

This special edition of the memoir of George Dorr has been prepared from the full text of the original works published by Dorr and his estate in 1942 and 1948. Additional illustrations and photographs, contemporaneous with the writings, have been added by the publisher to further illustrate the text.

COVER PHOTO

We would like to thank Deborah Dyer and the Bar Harbor Historical Society for the use of this unique archival photograph of George Dorr. Cover design by Julie Savage.

Third Edition - printed June 1997.

INTRODUCTION

How many millions of sightseers have travelled the paths and roads of Acadia National Park since its official establishment as a National Monument in 1916? No one knows for sure, but this year it is estimated that more than one and a half million people will make more than four million visits to this wonderland "where the mountains meet the sea." Of that vast number, few realize that the incredible beauty they are enjoying is the fulfillment of one man's dream. If it had not been for the lifelong commitment of George B. Dorr, the Park simply would not exist.

George Dorr, a bachelor with inherited wealth, was one of the original "rusticators" who made the island of Mount Desert his summer home. From his youth he had enjoyed, and taken for granted, the mountains and the sea of this famous resort community. Then, in the summer of 1901, he received a letter that would forever alter the course of his life.

President Eliot — Charles W. Eliot, the president of Harvard University for forty years and a prominent founder of the Northeast Harbor summer colony — wrote to Mr. Dorr requesting his assistance in the establishment of a committee "to hold reservations at points of interest on this Island, for the perpetual use of the public." This simple proposition grew rapidly in importance until it became the vocation, some would say the obsession, of Mr. Dorr. During the next forty-seven years of his life, Mr. Dorr would serve as the catalyst bringing men of wealth, politics, and power together at critical times in the evolution of Acadia. Under his constant guidance it would grow from a concept into a natural preserve covering more than 40,000 acres of Mt. Desert Island, much of Schoodic Peninsula on the mainland, and several of the surrounding islands.

In the early years of 1940 he was persuaded to set down in written form his recollections about the origin and development of the Park. This became Book I of his memoir. It soon became apparent, however, that more needed to be said. He began Book II with the intention of showing the efforts which were being expended to maintain the unique quality of life found here on the Island — the quality of life that had given birth to the Park in the first place. He lived to complete his memoir, but did not live long enough to see Book II published.

While some may argue about the historical accuracy of some of the dates and events which George Dorr relates in his books, the depth of his personal involvement and the crucial role he played in the creation of Acadia National Park are unquestionable. He truly earned the title of "the Father of Acadia."

Frank J. Matter
May 1991

Setting the Scene

Twenty thousand years ago the island that would be called Mount Desert was completely buried under the ice of the Wurm Glaciation. The glacial ice sheet that had slowly moved south to bury the land was so thick that at one time the summit of Cadillac Mountain (the highest point on the Atlantic coast) was under three-quarters of a mile of ice. As the ice moved to the sea, it gouged U-shaped valleys in the ridge that crossed the island. This broke the ridge into a series of peaks which we call mountains. Over the next three thousand years, the ice melted and retreated until the current surface of rugged granite, glacial lakes, and the Somes Sound fjord were exposed to the sun.

No one has recorded who first set foot on the island, but long before Champlain placed Mount Desert Island on the map, the area was a summer retreat. The Indians made their way here each spring to hunt, fish, and enjoy the cooling ocean breezes. In 1613, when the first Europeans (the Jesuits and their colonists) appeared offshore, it was the local Indian chief, Asticou, who convinced them to stay and attempt a settlement. This ill-fated French venture was quickly terminated by the English who carried off the would-be colonists and left the island once again in the hands of the Indians.

Following Wolfe's victory over the French on the Plains of Abraham (September 13, 1759), a treaty was completed which effectively signaled that the entire northeastern coast of America was open to English settlement. Immigrants in the hundreds began to sail east in search of "free" land. The governor of Massachusetts, Sir Francis Bernard, was quick to see the potential of this new land—both for his own personal gain, and for the opportunity it offered for Massachusetts to lay claim to the province of Maine. On February 27, 1762, the General Court of Massachusetts made a grant to the governor of one half of the island of Mount Desert (the western half). He immediately dispatched map makers and surveyors to his new holding to lay out a town and lots for the expected arrival of immigrants. When they arrived in October of 1762, they found two families already living on the Bernard property. Their records show that Abraham Somes was unboubtedly the pioneer settler on Mount Desert. Bernard and his survey crew made Southwest Harbor the center of their activity and designed lots around the favorable harbor there.

In the years just preceeding the Revolutionary War, colonists from Massachusetts made their way to the island and set up homesteads. They appear to have been subsistance farmers and fishermen. Although the onset of the Revolutionary War had little affect on the settlers, it brought disaster to Bernard. He was recalled to England and his estates were subsequently confiscated by Massachusetts.

In 1785, Bernard's son (who had been living in Bath, Maine) petitioned the Court of Massachusetts to regain his father's holdings on the island. This was granted, but the settlers were very unwilling to acknowledge a new owner of the land they had been working for years.

Another claimant to the island appeared in 1786. Madame Marie Therese de Gregoire (the grand-daughter of Antonie de la Motte Cadillac, who had been granted Mount Desert Island by the French crown in 1688) appeared at the General Court of Massachusetts to claim her inheritence. The General Court was disposed to recognize her claim due to the help Massachusetts had received from the French government during the recent war with England. If they had any doubts about recognizing her claim, they were totally removed when she produced evidence of support from both Lafayette and Thomas Jefferson. She was granted the whole eastern half of the island, except for those lots already occupied by "squatters." She sailed for the island and built her home in Hulls Cove. She continued to live there after the death of her husband. Their children abandoned the land and returned to England after her death in 1810.

In 1789 the entire island was incorporated as a town. The settlers, now called "locals," were fisherman, shipbuilders, and sea captains who eked out a living from the resources in and around the island. The center of activity remained Southwest Harbor. Occassional visitors such as yachtsmen, hunters, and adventurers brought news and cash money from the more populous New England states.

In 1844, the island was discovered by Thomas Cole, the founder of the famous Hudson River School of Art. He loved the rustic, wild beauty of the area and was soon bringing students here every year to paint and draw its fabulous landscape. The success of his work helped to popularize the island in the minds of his wealthy patrons. Perhaps due to the "commercialisation" of Southwest Harbor, the undeveloped beauty of the eastern half of the island (especially the area around Eden — Bar Harbor) became the focus of the new visitors' attention. By the 1860's, there were enough visitors to Eden each summer for the locals to add rooms to their houses and establish themselves as boarding houses. Still more tourists came and soon a new hotel was being built or expanded each year to accomodate not only the ever increasing number but also the more expensive tastes of the summer visitors. These visitors came for the "season" which generally extended from late June into September. At the peak of the so-called Hotel Era in the 1880's, Eden could boast of sleeping accomodations for nearly five thousand visitors. It also proudly told the world that it had the largest summer hotel in the nation — the Rodick House.

The season-long visitors, however, were having their problems. Daily steamship arrivals and the now daily train runs to Eden had greatly increased the number of casual visitors who came to spend a week or two on the island. These new intruders disrupted the summer routines in the hotels and restaurants. Letters to the editor of the local paper began to complain about these "tourists" who rushed everywhere trying to see the entire island in just a few weeks, who constantly moaned about a few days of bad weather, and who did not respect the slow, quiet pace that had been the norm on the island.

Mrs. H. D. Gibson's Summer Cottage "The Moorings"

The season-long visitors began to buy large tracts of land from the locals and build elaborate mansions, called "summer cottages," where they could continue with their summer activities hidden away from the hustle of the tourists. The scale of the building was impressive. The property valuation for the town of

Eden (Bar Harbor) grew from $622,901 in 1880 to $5,034,958 in 1890.

Mrs. R. B. Scott's Summer Cottage "Thirlstane"

At about this time, there was an increase in the number of amusements established for the tourists. The Indian encampment located at the foot of Bridge Street, just oppposite Bar Island, did a good business in sweet grass baskets, trinkets, and canoe rides around the outer islands. The retail district included branches of the most popular stores in the East. The hotels, now on the decline, offered dancing and other entertainment in the evenings. There was even a cog railway to the summit of Green Mountain (Cadillac Mountain). As the century was drawing to a close, there was an ever increasing pressure on the resources of the island and on the lifestyles of the summer residents.

The popularitiy of the area seemed to increase each year. This movement was aided by the increasing ease with which the casual visitor could reach the island. By the turn of the century, the introduction of the automobile threatened to escalate dramatically the number of people wishing to share in the delights of this now internationally famous resort community.

It was with these circumstances in mind that President Eliot wrote to George B. Dorr.

GEORGE BUCKNAM DORR AS A YOUNG MAN

ACADIA NATIONAL PARK
Its Origin and Background

George B. Dorr

Book I

FIRST PUBLISHED IN 1942

ACADIA NATIONAL PARK
Its Origin and Background

———————

I have been asked to tell how Acadia National Park came into being, took root and grew. Origins gain interest as events recede. Whatever changes come, the Park as a possession of the people will be as permanent, doubtless, as man's need for recreation and enjoyment of great coastal scenery. So, for the interest of the future, I will tell how the Nation came to own some dominant portions of this historic, mountainous and time-worn landscape, unique on our Atlantic coast.

But the story, if told at all, must needs be personal, for the creation of the Park from its inception on has been — and has had to be — a one man's job, though it sprang, as all things do, from antecedents that were, in their various degrees and combinations, its ultimate and real creators and hence form a necessary portion of the tale.

On August 12th, 1901, I received a letter from President Eliot, which read as follows:

Asticou, Maine
12 August, 1901

Dear Mr. Dorr,

I wrote to Mr. Parke Godwin, a week ago or more, asking him to appoint a committee from the Village Improvement Society of Bar Harbor to confer with committees from the Village Improvement Societies of Seal Harbor and North East Harbor touching the organization of a board of trustees or commission to hold reservations at points of interest on this Island, for the perpetual use of the public. Yesterday he wrote me a note, received this morning, from which it appears that he has not appointed any committee on behalf of the Village Improvement Society of Bar Harbor. Our conference is to be held tomorrow afternoon at four o'clock, at the Music Room on Rowland Road, Seal Harbor. Would it be possible for you and one or two other gentlemen from Bar Harbor to attend this conference in an unofficial capacity?

Mr. Godwin mentions that there is a meeting of your Village Improvement Society on the same day, but he does not state the hour.

I have written to him this morning a letter in which I set forth the objects which our Society had in mind proposing the conference, of which I enclose herewith a copy. I will explain to you the general purpose of the movement. I feel sure that you will sympathize with it. I approach the undertaking myself from the cottagers' point of view, but I believe it to be a measure on which all persons interested in the preservation of this Island as a place for healthful enjoyment could unite.

Very truly yours,

Charles W. Eliot

George B. Door, Esq.
Later.
I have just heard from Bishop Lawrence that you will attend the conference. Please bring some other gentlemen. C. W. E.

I got Mr. John S. Kennedy, Mr. George Vanderbilt and Mr. William Jay Schieffelin, neighbors of mine on the Bar Harbor shore, to accompany me to the meeting, Mr. Kennedy taking us over to Seal Harbor in his steam yacht which lay conveniently off his estate, Kenarden, bordering upon Cromwell's Harbor.

The Rt. Rev'd William Lawrence, Bishop of Massachusetts, drove over and met us at Seal Harbor. President Eliot was already awaiting us when we arrived, with the Rt. Rev'd William C. Doane, Bishop of Albany, and Mr. S. D. Sargent of Northeast Harbor, donor and builder of the Sargent Drive along the Somes Sound shore. There were also present the Rev'd William Adams

Brown and Professor Edward S. Dana, the geologist, of Seal Harbor, and, representing the then extensive David Dows-Cooksey interests at Seal Harbor, Mr. Richard M. Hoe and Mr. George L. Stebbins.

The meeting was called to order by President Eliot, who presided and stated its purpose. A vote to organize was passed and a committee to that end was appointed.

President Eliot became the Corporation's president; I, its vice-president and executive officer; George L. Stebbins, of Seal Harbor, treasurer; and Professor Lea McI. Luquer, of Bar Harbor, secretary. The firm of Deasy & Lynam, of Bar Harbor, became the Corporation's counsel; and the meeting adjourned, to reassemble at Bar Harbor on September 14th, 1901, where all future meetings, it was decided, would be held.

A charter was obtained when Maine's biennial Legislature next convened, January 1st, 1903, recognizing the public service character of our Corporation in making it free of tax.

The purpose of the Corporation as stated in its charter was "to acquire, by devise, gift or purchase, and to own, arrange, hold, maintain or improve for public use lands in Hancock County, Maine, which by reason of scenic beauty, historical interest, sanitary advantage or other like reasons may become available for such purpose."

Two gifts followed our incorporation: a rod square site on top of a bold cliff on the picturesque, ocean-fronting Cooksey Drive, whereon to establish a commemoration tablet recording the sailing past of Champlain, in September, 1604, in his exploration of the coast for the Sieur de Monts who had come out that spring with a commission from Henry IV of France, Henry of Navarre, to occupy 'the lands and territory of the region,' known to him from the accounts of fishermen and traders as Acadia; and a hilltop overlooking Jordan Pond, which was a favorite walk with the summer visitors at Seal Harbor.

For the following five years no other gifts were made, nor any effort to secure them; the Corporation slept.

In September, 1908, when I was laid up in my Storm Beach home at Bar Harbor, recovering from a surgical operation, President Eliot came to see me on his way home from the Trustees' annual meeting, for a friendly call and to bring me the news that the Trustees had received their first important gift, the Bowl and Beehive tract on Newport Mountain.

The Bowl, a picturesque little mountain lake, lies in a hollow surrounded by woods, four hundred feet above the sea; the Beehive is a bold headland beyond it to the south, overlooking the Sand Beach and Great Head, with the open sea beyond.

SAND BEACH AND THE BEEHIVE

The gift came from Mrs. Charles D. Homans of Boston, an old friend alike of my family's and President Eliot's, who had acquired the property a score or more of years before in the purchase of a site of great beauty on the shore below, on which to build.

It was a gift singularly appropriate to the Trustees' purpose, beautiful, unique and wild, and, welcoming it, I said to President Eliot that as soon as I got on my feet again I would see what I could do to get the summit of Green Mountain — Cadillac now, under the Government's re-naming — from the landscape point of view the one outstanding tract upon the Island or the whole neighboring coast to secure and protect if possible.

So, as soon as I did get about, I went, with this the first thought in mind, to my neighbor on the shore and older friend,

Mr. John S. Kennedy of New York, one of our original group in organizing the Trustees, and asked him if he would not help me acquire for them the summit of the mountain. For this the moment was singularly favorable, a great speculative enterprise involving it having come recently to its end, with nothing else to replace it as yet in sight.

To this he at once and most cordially agreed, and I, letting no grass grow under my feet, took steps forthwith to discover the owners of the summit tract — leased, not sold, to the promoters of the speculative enterprise I have just told of — and search out its bounds and title.

It proved a most interesting piece of work, and I still remember as though it were but yesterday the succession of beautiful Indian summer days I spent upon the mountain-top with my friend and legal assistant, Mr. Harry Lynam, tracing out and identifying the bounds of the land I sought.

This lay all comprised within a single lot, some eighty-five acres in extent, obtained by Daniel Brewer, of one of the early settler families of the town, from his father, Edward Brewer of Hulls Cove, who had himself purchased it along with a broad extent of forest-land below from the Bingham Heirs of Philadelphia, who held at that time vast stretches of wild forest-land in Eastern Maine invested in at the end of the last century for their timber value.

Daniel Brewer, with two others of his family in association with him, obtained this summit land for the purpose of building an inn upon it, when summer visitors first began to seek Bar Harbor out for its beauty's sake. All was very simple then and there was a sense of adventure about it which gave it zest. Into this Daniel Brewer's early mountain house, with its rough road for hauling people up, fitted well. But its day now was long since done.

In laying out the mountain top, Daniel Brewer and his associates had done a most complete and thorough job, including in its area every commanding point of view upon the whole broad summit, the highest and the boldest on our oceanfront, from Maine to Florida, and the central feature of Acadia National Park.

For the story of the next tract I got I must needs go back to the road I had built jointly with the Town, a dozen or so years before, to provide my mother and her older friends, who could not walk, with a short drive around the eastern and northern sides of the Great Meadow, there to connect with the old grassy road which led to Harden Farm and the former Leland mill-site on Kebo Brook, entering from Cromwell's Harbor Road.

At the foot of the long slope of Harden Farm one of the early cleared and cultivated farmlands of the Island, there issues a spring of pure, clear water, of constant flow but no great volume, and Farmer Harden having passed on, his nephew and heir, John Prescott, undertook to develop this commercially — Town water not yet having been brought in from Eagle Lake — building alongside it a pump-house and bottling works. All this cost money and a friendly Ellsworth financier advanced it, taking in security a mortgage on the spring and farm. The debt mounted through successive borrowings faster than returns came in and the lender, become less friendly now, foreclosed and took over to himself the farm and spring.

John Prescott now was out of it, but there was another and far greater spring sunk deep in the woods near the Great Meadow's southern end, which the old Indian trail along the foot of Flying Squadron Mountain passed by on its way to the Gorge and the oceanfront at Otter Creek. This was on land owned by the Rodick brothers, Fountain and Serenus, who with their father owned and operated during Bar Harbor's early resort period the largest hotel in the town, the Rodick House. From them Prescott now secured a lease, with option to purchase, on ten acres of the woodland where this spring flowed out, and, enlisting the aid of Ora Strout, active in the transportation business of the town, set out to develop the spring along the lines of the one he had lost at Harden Farm.

This spring was truly a magnificent one, well worthy of the development they planned, but such development costs money and presently John Prescott, unable to bear his share, turned over his interest in the lease to his associate, who himself soon after stopped, retaining in return for his expenditure the lease from the Rodick brothers and the unfinished building.

Springs, from boyhood on, have always held a singular interest for me, an interest heightened by years of travel abroad where, from the earliest historic period on, they have been objects of mystery and worship. And this spring was wonderfully placed, with the mountains rising steeply up beside it, contrasting with the Great and Little Meadow lands on either side. Hidden as it was by concealing woods, I had not realized its existence till Strout and Prescott's work began, but now that it had come to a halt, I set myself to see for what price it could be obtained and added to our Reservations. But the price was high, five thousand dollars, and there was no other purchaser in sight, so I let the matter lie, entering only into an agreement with Ora Strout not to sell to another without first giving me an opportunity to buy. And there the matter rested; there seemed no need for haste.

Then one fair spring morning in 1909, when I was out, here and there, looking after work I had in hand, Mr. Harry Lynam, knowing my interest in the tract, drove up hastily, out searching for me, and said:

"Mr. Dorr, a bunch of them up town have got together and raised the money to take over the option on the spring, which they believe to be essential to your plans. Ora Strout gives you until noon to take it, but will sell to them upon the stroke of twelve unless you close with him first. Cash in hand, they are waiting by the clock upon the Village Green till noon shall come to make the purchase. What will you do?"

This was in the old, slow horse-driving days. Mr. Lynam had spent some time in search for me and when he found me there was but a scant fifteen minutes left in which to reach the Village Green, a mile or more away. There was no time to spare. I made up my mind on the spot to take the option, and Mr. Lynam drove back as rapidly as the team which had brought him down could carry him, to so tell Mr. Strout. He found him waiting on the Village Green, where were also gathered the group that sought to take the option from me, waiting, cash in hand, for the hour to strike. When Mr. Lynam drove up, with but two or three minutes to spare, and told Mr. Strout that I would take it, they could not conceal their anger and hot words ensued between

SIEUR DE MONTS SPRING

them and Strout. But the spring was mine, and became, as it proved, one of the foundation stones on which the future Park was built.

Freeing it from a concealing cover of sphagnum moss and fallen leaves, which hid the full abundance of its flow, I shaped the sloping ground about it into a shell-like, concave basin, deeply draining it around to carry off all surface water from the mountainside above. I then built over it the octagonal, tiled-roof cover house, of old Florentine design, which is there today, with the arched openings upon the sides protected to a man's height and over with plates of purest glass, so that all who wished might look in and see the water gushing out in generous rush, to be led away by pipe to where the public might drink of it freely, if they would.

To the spring I gave the name of the founder of Acadia: The Sieur de Monts. And in memory of two spring-fountains I once had visited, on opposite shores of the Bosphorus, built by the Greeks in classic times and named by them, respectively, The Sweet Waters of Europe and The Sweet Waters of Asia, I called these waters, flowing out at the mountain base in such purity and abundance, The Sweet Waters of Acadia, carving this upon a granite rock I placed beside the spring.

Another tract that I got that year was the great granite block walling the Otter Creek Gorge upon the western side as Picket Mountain does upon the eastern. What I sought carried with it also the magnificent boulder-strewn ravine separating this from Cadillac Mountain, and beyond it, to the west, the high mountain slope connecting it unbrokenly with the lands on Cadillac Mountain summit I had acquired the year before and placed in the hands of the Trustees of Public Reservations.

For this I went to my friends of old New York and Lenox days, Mr. and Mrs. John Innes Kane, who had then recently, following the death of her father, William Schermerhorn, become summer residents at Bar Harbor, as had also Mrs. Kane's older sister, Mrs. William Bridgham, and her husband.

To them, lovers of our woodland walks and mountain climbs, the ravine I have described, the finest climb of such character upon the island, made strong appeal and they readily agreed, combining in the gift, the cost not being great and the two sisters having recently inherited a great fortune from their father.

The following fall, that of 1909, I set out to give the Trustees a tract of my own land, land of my inheritance from my father that was full of association for me. This was a tract where, following rains, Bear Brook comes tumbling down the ravine between Picket Mountain and Champlain to enter a basin at the bottom called Beaver Dam Pool from the relics of old beaver dams which it contained and the presence of an occasional beaver still to be seen swimming in it. A reedy margin surrounded it and giant hemlocks and yellow birches grew round about.

Around the pool and winding among the ancient forest trees, I had built, a dozen years before, for my friends' and the public's use, a broad bicycle path, at a time when when a new development of geared machines and rubber-tubed tires had given new popularity to the bicycle, and everyone who could was riding. My path found instant favor and people came down from the hotels and cottages in throngs to enjoy it, riding round and round, but not, as I had hoped they might, building others like it elsewhere to widen the opportunity and interest.

The Bicycle Path, just wide enough for my mother to pass through in her little one-horse buckboard, became a favorite drive for her in days of mellow autumn sunshine, where she could quietly watch the yellow birch leaves change and fall. But now, my mother gone, I wanted to make a gift to the public, through the Reservations, of this land in which she had found such happiness.

A MOUNTAIN VIEW

But Picket Mountain, with its bold, southward-facing cliff looking out across the sea, and some neighboring portions of Champlain Mountain which lay beyond my ownership were needed to complete the gift. For this I went to Mr. Kennedy, who once more most willingly agreed to aid. No papers passed between us; his word was enough. I promptly got in touch with the owners, who held the tract only for its lumber value, and made agreement with them for the purchase of the land. While I was still at work with them, searching out its bounds, Mr. Kennedy left for his winter home in New York. Soon I heard that he was ill of pneumonia; then word came suddenly that he had died. It was a great loss to me and I felt it deeply. It left me, also, in a difficult situation as regards the land he had offered to buy, for I had entered into a definite agreement with the owners for its purchase.

But it happened, most movingly to me, that the last words his wife had heard him utter, as she bent over him to hear what he might say, were: 'Remember . . . . that I promised Mr. Dorr . . . . to help him get that land.'

Legally, his executors could not recognize an unattested, spoken word; and it was not until the following spring that I received a check from them for the amount which he had pledged. But his thought of me and remembrance of that pledge in his last hours has remained with me always, a precious memory.

The next tract I got, most important in the development it led to, lay along the eastern shore of Eagle Lake. Chance brought the opportunity; I did not seek it. A prominent summer resident at Bar Harbor made plans to build, under the name of camp, a home at a beautiful point on the eastern shore of the lake. The only access to this site lay over an old wood-road skirting the lake-shore back of its fringing woods and leading on ultimately to Bubble Pond, where the owner of all the land it traversed, Martin Roberts, son of the earliest hotel-keeper at Bar Harbor, planned to build himself a camp where he could stay at will and keep open house for his friends — a plan which, happily, was never carried out. He had sold to the summer resident a site which lay between the old wood-road and the lake, where the shore, rising up, projected broadly out toward the west, with a beautiful view over the whole lake basin. But there was no opportunity to drain the building away from the lake, whose waters, drawn from a high level, supplied the whole town, and whose purity had hitherto been its greatest asset.

The sale was made quietly. Work on construction was not commenced until late fall, when all summer residents had left; as it lay off the public road, no notice was taken of the building until in the early winter an enthusiastic account of it as a new development appeared in the local weekly paper, which, subscribed to by the year, reached all summer residents in their winter homes. The reaction that followed was not at all what the editor had anticipated; but there was plenty of it.

Mr. John S. Kennedy, who out of public spirit had purchased and re-organized the earlier water company, a native undertaking, had, as I have elsewhere told, died that fall, but the Directors of the Company, chosen at that time from leading summer residents, promptly met in New York and decided that the construction of the projected building must be stopped at any cost. I was not a member of that board, but all knew my interest in what concerned Bar Harbor, and their chairman, Mr. William Lee, was instructed to write me in Boston asking if I, as nearest to the scene, would not run down to Bar Harbor, look the situation over, and see what could be done.

Recognizing at once the importance of the matter and the broad issues it involved, I packed my bag and took the night train down, taking with me, in addition to the authority to act for the Directors, a letter from Dr. Robert Abbe, famous New York surgeon, who had been serving most efficiently the last few years as chairman of the Bar Harbor Village Improvement Association's sanitary committee and who denounced the project in no uncertain terms.

Arriving at the Ferry and taking the stout little steamboat which butted its way through the ice across the Upper Bay, I went directly, on reaching Bar Harbor, to talk the matter over with the president of the Water Company, Mr. Fred C. Lynam, and told him of the authority given me by the Directors to represent them in the matter. His first reaction was that nothing could be done at that late stage to stop construction — the work had gone too far, the cost would be too great. I then showed him Dr. Abbe's letter and told him of the instruction I had received from him to print it, were the project to go on. He read it and

Eagle Lake

VIEW OF EAGLE LAKE

exclaimed: "For God's sake, don't print that letter!" I replied that I must, were construction to continue.

Finally it was settled that the summer resident for whom the house was being built should be communicated with to see whether, and upon what terms, he would consent to give the project up; and the Secretary of the Water Company was dispatched to get in touch with him.

Found in Florida, he reluctantly gave the project up, the Company agreeing to repay him his expenditure upon the land, assuming the ownership and compensating the contractor.

This incident, with its large expenditure for a single tract, full three times what it might have been purchased for had it been taken in season, served as a valuable object lesson on the importance of anticipating other undertakings of the kind such as now were likely, with the high price to stimulate them, to spring up over the whole drainage basin of the lake.

The Bar Harbor Water Company had then no condemnation rights for the protection of its supply and any owner of land draining to the lake could hold the Company up for whatever price he might choose to ask, with the sky the limit, by threatening to build upon it. The Water Company had sought to obtain such rights at the time of its incorporation but the State Legislature, moved by fear of the use that might be made of them by a business corporation, had refused to grant them. Learning this, it occurred to me that where the Company had failed, I, acting for the Trustees of Public Reservations, with none but the public interest to serve, might be able to secure these rights; at all events, no harm to try.

Among Bar Harbor's then rapidly increasing summer population were, besides Dr. Abbe, leading physicians nationally known, while at Seal Harbor Professor William T. Sedgwick of the Massachusetts Institute of Technology, recognized as the first authority in America on sanitation, made his summer home and I knew him well.

I knew, too, that I could count on the solid support of the great body of summer residents and taxpayers of Mount Desert Island eastward from Somes Sound, and I entered my bill, in the name of the Trustees of Public Reservations, sweepingly to cover the whole Island. What I got was the power granted to our Trustees to condemn, on evidence of importance shown, the connected watersheds of Eagle Lake and Jordan Pond.

These powers obtained, the Directors of the Bar Harbor Water Company forthwith requested me to acquire, in the name of the Trustees of Public Reservations, all land within the drainage basin of the Lake which the Company's reserve funds, then considerable from the original sale of stock, permitted. On this the Company expended $65,000, leaving only certain areas, more costly than the rest, at the foot of the Lake where the public highway runs close by, lower than the intake of the Lake, for later acquisition. These, too, were purchased later and added to the rest, after the National Park was founded, completing the protection of the waters of the Lake from all contamination to the incalculable benefit, alike in fact and reputation, not only of Bar Harbor but the whole wide territory the Bar Harbor Water Company serves.

The interest aroused by our accomplishment for the Public Reservations in the Bar Harbor region did not pass until it resulted in a like achievement at Seal Harbor, where the mountains either side of Jordan Pond, the most beautiful sheet of water on the Island, and the green, rounded Bubbles which separate its basin from that of Eagle Lake all were added, together with the whole western slope of Cadillac Mountain below the actual summit portion I had already secured.

The problem here was greatly simplified by the purchase, for some few hundred dollars, by an early, enthusiastic summer visitor at Bar Harbor, Mr. Charles T. How, of Jordan Mountain, with its Cedar Swamp Mountain spur, the amphitheater between, and the high south slope of Sargent Mountain beyond. With them he acquired too, for land there had little value at that time, the grassy sward at the foot of Jordan Pond, where he used to stage great picnics for guests, numbered sometimes by the hundred, who sat upon the grass with cloths spread out in lieu of tables, and with a delightful spirit of freedom and enjoyment over all. That was the time of hotels, great and small, at Bar Harbor, where summer residential life had scarce begun. Excursions were the order of the day and many drove out by buckboard to Schooner Head and Great Head, for as yet the Ocean Drive did not exist.

Mr. How was a real institution of Bar Harbor's summer life in those days, adding greatly with his exuberant spirit and entertaining talk to the "gaiety of nations." For him How's Park, in the valley below Great Hill, is named, with the monument to him at its entrance placed there by friends in memory of those early days.

These lands around the basins of Eagle Lake and Jordan Pond, connecting and forming together a single whole, with their beauty and importance to the public health, added to the mountain slopes and summits we had now secured, made a splendid holding for our Trustees of Public Reservations and on it in achievement we could, I thought, fairly afford to rest.

At the beginning of January, 1913, I was at my home in Boston, with every intention of spending the winter there, when the telephone rang and, answering it, I found on the line Mr. Harry Lynam, my friend and legal assistant at Bar Harbor, who said:

"Mr. Dorr, I think you will wish to know that a group of them down here have got together and have introduced a bill in the State Legislature, now just convened at Augusta, to annul the charter of our Trustees of Public Reservations corporation."

Answering, I said: "I will take the train down to Augusta tonight. Meet me there tomorrow and we will see what can be done."

Arriving at Augusta, I went straight to the Augusta House, where, during sessions, practically all members of the Legislature make their home, the hotel becoming in effect a club where the members meet and talk together, visiting about from room to room, when the Legislature is not in session or committee meetings being held.

As it chanced, my friend, the Hon. John A. Peters of Ellsworth, was Speaker of the House that year. He had aided me professionally in various matters at Bar Harbor and I knew him well. I told him what had brought me down and he took the matter up at once with interest, realizing its importance. He made me at home in his rooms at the hotel, where his friends and members of the House came to talk the business of the session over, and together, at other times, we went about ourselves and visited leading members who might have influence in our matter. In fact, we made a most thorough campaign of it, winning friends and votes so that when, ten days or so later, our bill came up for hearing the action of the committee on it was a foregone conclusion.

The representative from Bar Harbor, questioned by the Committee, had himself no good word to say for the measure, stating that he had not entered the bill of his own initiative but at the request of others, and added that, personally, he did not favor it.

In bringing about the defeat of this measure, much water had flowed beneath the bridge since I came down; it had been a new experience to me and made me realize on how unstable a basis our Reservations rested.

Returning that night to Boston, I thought it over as I lay awake and decided that the only course to follow to make safe what we had secured would be to get the Federal Government to accept our lands for a National Park, deeming them well worth it. In the morning, having breakfasted, I went out to Cambridge to see President Eliot and tell him what had happened — for as yet he knew nothing of the matter nor the danger that had threatened. I told him also of the thought of how to meet it that had come to me that night as I returned.

President Eliot was at first opposed, being naturally of a militant mind, and said that we could meet such attacks as they arose, as the University had done when the city of Cambridge undertook to tax its lands and buildings. To this I replied that the cases were widely different; that the University had back of it a great and influential body of alumni, while in our case if Mr. Lynam had not been on the watch and let me know what was going on and I had not been able and willing, dropping all else, to go down to Augusta and, with Mr. Peters' friendly assistance, defeated the attack, all, even now, would have been lost. He thought a while, then said:

"I believe you are right! When will you go on to Washington?"

It is here that the story of our National Park begins, born of the attack upon our Public Reservations' charter.

A few weeks after my talk with President Eliot, I went on to Washington, timing my visit to coincide with the coming in of the new administration under President Wilson, inaugurations then still taking place upon the traditional March 4th.

I took up my stay there with my friend Gifford Pinchot, until a short time before Chief of the Forest Service and its founder under Theodore Roosevelt. He had been recently in the limelight for his support of the Glavis charges against Secretary of the Interior Ballinger for rental at a nominal sum to a private corporation of the Government's coal fields in Alaska. In joining Glavis in these charges, Gifford Pinchot, resigning his position as head of the Forest Service, had employed as counsel Louis D. Brandeis, future member of the United States Supreme Court, famous, in company with Justice Oliver Wendell Holmes, for liberal interpretation of the law and the Constitution.

Pinchot, a close friend of Theodore Roosevelt, had been one of the chief factors in causing the rift between Roosevelt and Taft which resulted in the formation of the Bull Moose party and opened the way for the election to the presidency of Woodrow Wilson, a Democrat, through the splitting of the Republican ranks.

Gifford Pinchot, a bachelor still, lived with his parents in a big double house they had built for themselves and him, and there, soon after my coming, they gave a reception in honor to members of President Wilson's incoming cabinet, whom I thus met under pleasantest conditions.

It was a most interesting time to be in Washington, with discussion of President Wilson's new policies everywhere in the air and the echoes of party strife still ringing. I made a stay of some length, getting in touch with people and learning from one and another what was going on politically beneath the surface.

One occasion during that visit comes back to me outstandingly as I write, when Secretary of the Interior Franklin K. Lane and Mrs. Lane gave a dinner al fresco one pleasant afternoon at the Old Mill Restaurant in Rock Creek Park in honor to Secretary of the Treasury McAdoo and his bride, the former Eleanor Wilson, daughter of the President, when we dined under a canopy of springtime foliage among the tall trunks of deciduous trees to the music of the full-flowing creek.

Another occasion I specially recall during that visit to the Pinchots was a dinner at the home of the Hon. Henry White, to which I, an old friend of his wife, Daisy Rutherford, whom I had known in my boyhood days at Newport, had been bidden. The dinner was given in honor to William Jennings Bryan, then recently appointed Secretary of State under President Wilson. With it is connected, in my memory, a story of not a little human interest.

Henry White, of Baltimore, called the first 'Career Diplomat' of the United States, had married, a score or more of years before, Margaret Stuyvesant Rutherford, the daughter of Lewis Morris Rutherford of New York, a man of inherited fortune, who, devoting himself to astronomy, had become one of the leading authorities in the world on spectroscopy and photography of the stars. In connection with the latter, there comes back to me the memory of a magnificent great photograph of the surface of the moon which Mr. Rutherford had presented to my mother when she and my father dined with him and his wife one evening while on a visit to New York, and when they were shown the moon itself through his great telescope. This photograph, brought back to Boston by my mother, became one of the wonders of my childhood.

Entering on his career as diplomat after his marriage, Henry White, following a brief service at Vienna, had become, and long remained, Secretary of our Legation at London; then, after an interval, of our newly established Embassy there, the first that the United States sent out. During their service in England he and his wife had won for themselves a unique position among the old and generally exclusive English aristocracy and society at large.

Now comes my tale, and with it explanation of the Henry Whites' residence in Washington at that time and the dinner I attended, given in honor to the "Great Commoner," Secretary of State Bryan.

Judge Taft, already a man of note, had married, at the time of Mr. White's earlier secretarial service at London, and gone abroad with his wife on their honeymoon, making their first stay in London. While they were there, he wrote our Legation asking for tickets to hear a notable debate in Parliament. Unfortunately, his letter fell to some subordinate in the Legation to take charge of who made reply that tickets for that particular debate had been much sought and that none remained at their disposal, but in their stead he enclosed tickets for Judge Taft and his wife to visit the Royal Mews! Accidental and humorous though this was, the Tafts never forgot nor forgave it, so the story ran. And when Taft in due course followed Theodore Roosevelt as President, one of his earliest acts was to put an end to Henry White's long diplomatic service.

Upon this, returning to America the Whites had bought themselves a beautiful home with spacious grounds about it high up on Sixteenth Street, whence, from rising ground, there was a wonderful view down the length of the street southward across Lafayette Square to the White House, with the Potomac and its broad parklands in the background. There, making their home the center of much gracious hospitality and ambitious still for further diplomatic service, they waited to see what the future might bring. This explains the dinner they were then giving for Mr. Bryan. For President Wilson, untrained as he was in diplomatic usage and the ways of diplomats, Henry White's long experience abroad was a god-send and he was presently to recognize it in a notable way by taking him with him to the Versailles Conference for consultation and advice.

Bryan, whom I met for the first and only time at that dinner, was one of the most extraordinary phenomena of his time, made famous by a single speech, the Cross of Gold Speech, as it was called, delivered extemporaneously before the Democratic National Convention at Chicago in 1896, which stampeded the convention and brought him from the floor — neither seeking nor desiring it — the nomination for the Presidency, on the issue of Free Silver. Ever afterward, though but thirty-six years old at the time, he remained an important national figure, swaying elections which he himself could not win, and giving weight to causes which, like those of the Volstead Act and Fundamentalism, would have had none without him.

Returning to the dinner at the Henry Whites, the occasion had for me, Bryan apart, interesting and amusing features. The dinner itself, given by the Whites, with their broad cultural background, for Bryan, editor of The Commoner, Fundamentalist of the olden time, and Free Silver man, was one such. Another I was made to realize by the complaint of Charles Francis Adams, whom I chanced to sit next at the dinner, that it was 'too dry' — he could not get his wine-glass refilled, which he felt as a real grievance at the moment. In this the dinner was a compromise, for Bryan, whom our host and hostess wished especially to please, was a complete teetotaler and a leader in the movement for prohibition; while Adams, naturally of an impatient temper, followed the old tradition of New England hospitality, by which wine — good wine — was served regularly as an essential feature at all formal dinners.

To get Mr. Adams off his grievance, I asked him why he had left Boston and come to Washington to take up his home. Whereupon he launched out into a diatribe upon the change for the worse that had taken place, since his earlier days, in Boston society, declaring, to my pleasure, that the one house in Boston to which he, at the last, could come to dine and count on good talk, good food and interesting people was my mother's. Then the champagne came round again and his grievances were forgotten.

I made a stay of some length in Washington, interested in the scenes, getting in touch with people, and learning from one and another what was going on politically beneath the surface.

But spring was now opening in the north and I returned to Boston and thence to Bar Harbor to gather my papers together and prepare the way for the offer of our Reservations lands to the Government, which would involve, I knew, no little work by Mr. Harry Lynam, my legal assistant, and myself.

The next spring, that of 1914, I went on to Washington with deeds, maps and abstracts of title to submit to the Government. There was no Park Service at that time, the Act creating it not being passed until August 25, 1916. Yellowstone Park was then still under the charge of the War Department, with a troop of cavalry to guard it, as it had been when I visited it a dozen years before on my way back from a trip to the Pacific coast and summer in the high Sierras. Such other parks as existed at that time were cared for individually in one way or another, as the history of their creation dictated or opportunity best served.

Under the Department of the Interior, what work there was to be done relating to National Parks was looked after by two young lawyers from the west: Horace M. Albright, a recent graduate from the University of California, who had come — temporarily only, as his intention was — to Washington to gain some knowledge of Federal procedure in regard to mining properties; and Joseph P. Cotter, who, afterwards, on Secretary Lane's withdrawing from the Government service, betook himself to Doheny, the oil operator, and with him continued, doing well and prospering, as I later understood. They, with two young women clerks to aid them, were quartered in a single room in the old Patent Office Building on F Street, housing at that time the Department of the Interior.

When I went on to Washington, Edward Howe Forbush, Massachusetts State Ornithologist and widely known the country over as a leading authority on bird life, accompanied me to urge acceptance of our offer for the much-needed protection it would afford to bird life, sea and land alike, at a most outstanding point on the coast of Maine.

Together, we went at once upon arrival to find Mr. Frank Bond, permanent executive secretary of the Public Lands Commission, to which in the first instance our offer and deeds would be submitted for examination and report. Mr. Bond was, in his leisure hours, a devoted student of bird life, maintaining a well-guarded sanctuary for them at his pleasant country home outside Washington, and hence was from the start in full sympathy with our project.

Dr. T. S. Palmer, experienced legislative contact agent of the Biological Survey, Department of Agriculture, was an old friend of Dr. Forbush and when we had found Mr. Bond, housed also in the old Patent Office Building upon F Street, we got him to come over and talk with us. Our mission told and the lands I had come on to offer described, Dr. Palmer, familiar as no one else with the shifting situation 'on the Hill' in regard to all matters relating to Wild Life, said:

"I can see at once how valuable this would be to bird life on our eastern coast, other aspects apart, but Congress is already loaded up with bills for the establishment of National Parks the country over, all calling for appropriations, and most of them, introduced solely for political effect, ought not to pass. You ask for no appropriation and offer something that is really valuable. But all the more, these other projects will be tacked onto yours in an omnibus bill and the whole go down to defeat."

"What then can I do?" I asked; "what have you to suggest?"

He then told me of the National Monuments Act, passed under Theodore Roosevelt in 1906, giving the President power to take from the National domain, set aside by proclamation and place under Federal control any tract of 'exceptional historic, prehistoric, scientific or scenic interest' whose conservation should be recommended to him by any one of certain designated members of his Cabinet — the Secretary of War, the Secretary of Agricultural, the Secretary of the Interior, and one or two besides; while a special clause had, happily for us, been added to include gifts from a private source in order to enable President Roosevelt to accept a noble stand, some four hundred odd acres in extent, of the Coastal Redwoods — Sequoia sempervirens — north of the entrance to San Francisco Bay, which John Muir, the famous naturalist and lover of the Sierra forest, had raised a fund to purchase and present to the Government.

This as a precedent so exactly fitted our case, though what we had to offer was on a greater scale, that I at once, on my own responsibility, assuming President Eliot's and the Trustees' concurrence, decided to follow it and ask the Government to accept our tract in free gift as a National Monument.

In following Dr. Palmer's advice, no action by Congress would be required; acceptance lay wholly with the President and the authorized member of his Cabinet recommending it to him — in our case, the Secretary of the Interior, Franklin K. Lane, whom I had met so pleasantly the year before and upon whose friendship and interest I knew already we could count.

Among his assistant secretaries, of whom there were several, was a classmate at the University of California, Stephen Tyng Mather, descendant of the famous old Mather family of the Massachusetts Bay Colony, a fact in which he took great interest and pride. Under him it was that the immediate charge of our lands would fall if accepted by the Government; but at the moment it was the Public Lands Commission only with whom I had to deal.

I turned over, accordingly, to Mr. Bond our deeds for examination by the legal officials of the Public Lands Commission, who held them for an unconscionable time as it seemed to me, waiting impatiently for their report. At last they were returned, accompanied by a brief statement telling me that while naught seemed wrong in them, they did not come up to the National

Government's exacting standard, and also that for the purpose of our offer two further tracts of land, indicated on a map I had submitted with our deeds, should be acquired to enable the tract presented to be bounded by a single line.

On this I returned to Boston and went out to see President Eliot at his home in Cambridge to talk the situation over. Until then all survey and legal expense connected with my work I had borne myself, but this new requirement, one leading on as it did to so definite a gain, I felt it only fair that others, cooperating with me, should assume. So, too, felt President Eliot and said he thought he might be able to obtain the sum needed from one or another of the great public trusts to whose management and high standing before the public he had devoted himself since, after forty years as its President, he had retired from Harvard.

This settled, I went back to Bar Harbor to arrange for purchasing the additional lands the Government had asked to have acquired and give what aid I could to Mr. Lynam in his study of the deeds.

But before I go on further with my story of the Park some word, brief though it be, must needs be said upon the change, swift and sudden, which had swept over the whole face of the earth since I had returned from Washington. Over it there now loomed the tremendous background of the first World War.

Of this, the first knowledge that came to me, immersed in my work, was when, early one mid-August morning I was dressing by the open window of my big sea-room at Oldfarm, overlooking the Bay, when, swiftly and silently, there came steaming into view the great German passenger liner, the Kronprincessen Cecile, which, proceeding on into the harbor, dropped anchor there and came to rest, discharging her passengers.

What had happened I was soon to learn. She had turned about when, as she was nearing her home port, word reached her commander of the declaration of war between Germany and England on August 4th, 1914, and raced full speed back across the Atlantic to seek shelter in neutral waters of the United States, the first within reach being those of Frenchman Bay where, off Bar Harbor, she came to rest.

On June 28th, 1914, the Archduke Francis Ferdinand of Austria was slain at Sarajevo, capital of Bosnia-Hercegovina, by a Serbian nationalist, and Austria, combining opportunity with vengeance, served on Serbia a four days' ultimatum, impossible for her to accept without sacrificing all sovereignty and independence as a State. And on July 28th, Austria opened war upon her. On this Russia, racial and traditional protector of the Serbs, commenced mobilization of her forces against Austria. Thereupon Kaiser Wilhelm II of Germany, who wanted but the long-waited opportunity this gave, marched his troops at once, under plans long prepared, through the treaty-guaranteed Grand Duchy of Luxembourg and on through Belgium, treaty-guaranteed as well, to the invasion of France, on the ground of her alliance with Russia, declaring war upon her only when actually on the way and after laying siege to and storming the old city of Louvain with it famous University library, whose buildings and priceless collection of manuscripts went up in flames, to be mourned by scholars still the whole world over.

In breaking their solemn pledge to respect the independence and inviolability of Luxembourg and Belgium, the Kaiser and his councillors had not counted on the resentment this would cause in England, too much occupied, they thought, with her own affairs to take part in matters across the Channel. In this they were wrong. The day of the announcement of Germany's war on France was in England 'such as no one within the memory of living man had ever known,' but the decision to move to the support of France as by treaty bound was practically unanimous in England and an expeditionary force was sent, without delay, to join with the French army in defense of the realm.

In coming to this decision, Sir Edward Goschen, Britain's ambassador to Berlin, was instructed to make announcement of it to the German Foreign Office, where the German Imperial Chancellor, Bethmann-Hollweg, expressed himself as greatly disturbed. It was utterly without cause, he declared.

"Just for a word — neutrality—" he said, "just for a 'scrap of paper' Great Britain is going to make war on a kindred nation who desires nothing better than to be friends with her."

But speed and the unpreparedness of her foe, taken by surprise, entered fundamentally into Germany's campaign plan and her army of invasion, under General von Kluck, swept on toward Paris with a force that seemed irresistible as cabled accounts of it came back to us in America, hanging breathless on the news, till Paris itself seemed on the verge of falling.

Then came the 'Miracle of the Marne' — miracle indeed it seemed. Joffre, French general in command, held back beyond all hope and expectation the onrushing German forces at the crossing of the river, while General Gallieni, in command at Paris, rushed every soldier he felt he could spare, or able-bodied citizen, in taxi-cabs, so close was now the scene of battle, out to the support of Joffre, while the British general, Sir John French, with his forces, anticipating von Kluck, with scarce an hour to spare at the crossing of the Ourcq, threatened the German forces from the North. And the retreat began, at the very hour when victory had seemed so near, under orders from German General Headquarters. Von Kluck had outmarched his support and the British juncture with the French endangered the whole German army. The swift, long-planned attack had failed and the impasse of trench warfare, with its surgings to and fro and interminable delays, had commenced.

In the meantime, my work with Harry Lynam on our Public Reservations deeds and papers had gone forward steadily, and with a thoroughness of research on his part which gave us both great confidence in the result. But work of such a character takes time and it was not until the spring of 1916, two years after my first offer had been made, that I felt justified in going on again to Washington, when the report was acclaimed by Mr. Bond as the finest piece of work of the kind that had ever come into his office. He further said that he felt he could advise the Public Lands Commission that in his opinion it called for no examination in detail — it might safely be accepted as it stood. And with this the committee's solicitor, looking at the mass of our material, thankfully agreed.

These titles, I may say in passing, formed in themselves a real historic study. Mr. Lynam, becoming deeply interested in the work, traced his records back to the first beginnings of land occupation or ownership in our region.

VIEW FROM SALISBURY COVE — THE COUNTRYSIDE CHOSEN BY THE EARLY SETTLERS OF EDEN

The earliest of all, legally speaking, was when Antoine de la Mothe Cadillac, soldier of fortune in the Acadian service but of ancient lineage in France, obtained a grant from the Province of Quebec — still on record in its archives — giving him in true feudal style the Lordship or Seigneurie of the Isle of Mount Desert, together with two square leagues upon the opposite mainland, a grant which presently, revisiting France, he obtained formal confirmation of from Louis XIV. Afterward, returning to America, he lived for a time, an old record tells, upon the Island's eastern shore — where Hulls Cove is now, most probably. But his home there being wrecked in a sea-raid from Massachusetts Bay, he, though still signing his deeds as 'Seigneur des Monts Deserts,' removed to Canada, offering his services to Frontenac and becoming presently, by his own initiative and enterprise, the founder of Detroit — "The City on the Strait."

Later, Acadia, lost to France on the battlefields of Europe through the generalship of Marlborough, was ceded to England in the Peace of Utrecht, in 1713, but still remained a scene of border warfare till the capture, by a combined English fleet and Colonial troops from the Province of Massachusetts Bay, of the strong fortress of Louisburg on Cape Breton in 1758, and the taking of Quebec the following year, when Wolfe fell in the storming of the Heights of Abraham.

Three years after this, in 1762, the General Court of the Province of Massachusetts Bay granted the western portion of the Island of Mount Desert, as divided by Somes Sound, to the Province's then popular governor, Sir Francis Bernard, who sailed down soon after in a Government vessel from Castle William, on one of the islands in Boston Harbor, to visit it, bringing with him surveyors and a considerable suite and laying out the town of Southwest Harbor for sale, in in-lots of eight and out-lots of forty acres, to settlers.

In the bitter strife, however, that preceded the outbreak of the Revolutionary War, Sir Francis lost his popularity with the people, taking the British side and adopting measures that led to a committee of influential Boston citizens waiting on him in protest at his beautiful home on the banks of Jamaica Pond.

"On this committee there served John Hancock, James Otis, Joseph Warren, Samuel Adams, and Josiah Quincy. It is a curious illustration of orderly rebellion when we picture this committee proceeding to Jamaica Plain in a procession of eleven chaises to call upon the governor. He received them courteously, offered them cakes and wine, and made them promises which he apparently did not mean to keep." *

The following year, feeling himself endangered by the popular resentment, he sailed for England, departing amid the rejoicing of the people, the ringing of bells and the firing of cannon.

His property in America — his grant of one-half of the Island of Mount Desert, and his stately mansion on the shore of Jamaica Pond — was confiscated afterward by the Province, on the outbreak of the Revolutionary War. But when the war was over and the Province of Massachusetts Bay had become a state, Sir Francis' son, John Bernard, who had remained quietly settled in the District of Maine during the Revolutionary struggle, came before the Massachusetts General Court and petitioned that his father's confiscated half-interest in the Island of Mount Desert be

*From **Mount Desert—A History** by George E. Street, first published in 1905.

MOUNT DESERT ISLAND FROM THE SEA

confirmed to him, and the Court, feeling perhaps that it might have dealt too harshly with the father, granted his request.

Soon after this, the granddaughter of Cadillac and her husband, M. and Mme. de Gregoire, fleeing the Revolution impending them in France, sailed out to Boston — a long journey in those days — and petitioned in turn the General Court to grant them her grandfather's possession in the Island of Mount Desert, seeking it not by claim of legal right but on grounds of sentiment — the aid that France had given the American colonies in their struggle for independence; and the Court, in like spirit, recognizing their claim as valid, gave them the yet ungranted eastern half of the Island, whither they came and settled at Hulls Cove, where, in the old cemetery, they now lie buried.

To these two grants, to Governor Bernard's son and Cadillac's granddaughter and her husband, all deeds to lands upon the Island trace back, save only those already at that time settled on which were excepted from the grants.

Two surveyors were soon after sent down to designate and record these lots, Salem Towne for the western half of the Island

and John Peters for the eastern. To these surveys it is that Mr. Lynam's studies, at their earliest, extended back.

For the National Monument we were seeking as our first step toward park-hood, I took the name of the founder of Acadia, the Sieur de Monts, within whose territory as granted him by Henry IV of France, Henry of Navarre, France's great warrior king, our Island and its whole surroundings, as far as to the Penobscot River, clearly lay.

Our deeds approved, my offer of our Reservation lands, addressed in due form to the Secretary of the Interior, the Hon. Franklin K. Lane, to forward to the President with his recommendation that it be accepted, follows:

PIERRE DU GUAST, SIEUR DE MONTS

To the Secretary of the Interior, Washington, D. C.

Sir:

On behalf of the Hancock County Trustees of Public Reservations, State of Maine, I have the honor to offer in free gift to the

United States a unique and noble tract of land upon our eastern seacoast, for the establishment of a National Monument.

The tract offered is rich in historic association, in scientific interest and in landscape beauty. Approximately five thousand acres in extent, it contains within itself the only heights that immediately front the open sea with mountainous character upon our eastern shore.

It contains also, owing to past glacial action and its own variously resistant rocky structure, an extraordinary variety of topographic features which unite with the climate caused by the surrounding sea to fit it beyond any other single locality in the east for the shelter, growth and permanent preservation of a wide range of life, both plant and animal. It forms a striking and instructive geologic record. And it constitutes the dominant and characteristic portion of the first land, Mount Desert Island, to be visited, described and named by Champlain when sailing under de Monts' orders in exploration of the New England coast.

The papers I enclose herewith will explain in more detail the thought and purpose of the offered gift, with the reasons which led us to conviction of its exceptional public value and worthiness to be accepted.

The bound volumes of report upon the deeds by which the offered lands are held represent the long labor of one of the most competent and well-versed legal firms in Maine, whose thoroughness of investigation may be relied upon with safety.

I remain, Sir, with respect,

Sincerely yours,

George Bucknam Dorr

May 3, 1916

These papers dispatched, what more remained to do rested with the Secretary, who promptly did his part, enclosing them with a letter of approval to the President with a proclamation prepared for the signature of the President, as the act required. And we waited his reply.

FRANKLIN K. LANE, SECRETARY OF THE INTERIOR, 1913-20

Days, then weeks, went by and still no answer came. In the meantime, I arranged for an interview with President Wilson to explain our offer and its purpose. To this I went accompanied by Senator Johnson of Maine, Representative John A. Peters, and one or two besides. When the President came in to greet us, I told him briefly our story and showed him a number of striking photographs taken by a noted landscape photographer whom I had brought down to Bar Harbor for the purpose. And as I did so, I told him something of the early history of the region and its human interest. He was friendly and kept us longer than we had anticipated; then, as we rose to leave, I said:

"Mr. President, I have taken much interest in your selection of Louis Brandeis for the Supreme Court Bench. I have known him for years in Boston and believe you could not have made a better choice."

On this he stopped, as he was accompanying us to the door, and kept us quite a time, talking of Brandeis, who on more than one occasion, he said, had saved him by wise counsel from serious mistakes, and of whom he though most highly. Brandeis at that time was being bitterly assailed in connection with the appointment and my praise of him, wholly sincere, was plainly welcome to the President.

Still no acknowledgment coming of Secretary Lane's letter to the President, with its accompanying draft of the Proclamation creating the Sieur de Monts National Monument, I grew uneasy and asked Charles Hamlin, an old Boston friend, who President Wilson had appointed Governor of the newly set up Federal Reserve Board, to take me over to the White House for a friendly call on Mrs. Wilson to invite her and the President down to stay with me at Oldfarm, as it was then already early summer, and view the new National Monument, thinking in this way to sound the matter out. Governor Hamlin readily consented and after lunch one day we went across from his offices in the Treasury Building to the White House, he having made appointment with Mrs. Wilson to receive us. Entering the reception room, and announced, she came in to greet us and I at once extended to her my invitation.

"But," she said — for she and the President had evidently spoken of it at lunch — "the President says that he does not feel sure he would be legally justified in signing that Proclamation."

On this, without more ado than courtesy required, I left, Governor Hamlin accompanying me, and went at once to my friends in the Interior Department, Albright and Cotter. Telling them what had happened, I asked:

"What does this mean?"

"It means," they said, "that the Forest Service has been knifing us!"

"I can not think that," I replied, "for when I first brought the matter up two years ago and spoke of my plan to Director Graves" — friend of Gifford Pinchot and following him as chief of the Forest Service — "he greeted it most warmly. But I will step across and see."

The Forest Service, extensive as its offices later came to be, then occupied only a single suite of rooms in a building upon F Street, nearly opposite the old Patent Office building where the Department of the Interior had its quarters at that time.

Director Graves I found in his office, and, without telling him what had happened at the White House, said, to feel out my way, that the plan of which I had told him two years before for a Federal reservation on the coast of Maine was coming up to be acted on and that I would like, if he were willing, to have from him in writing what he had then said so cordially in regard to it.

"Certainly," he said, "I'll be glad to do it!" And calling in a stenographer he dictated on the spot a letter in warm approval of the project. With this in evidence I returned to my friends in the Interior Building, who on reading it acknowledged that they had been wrong. But events showed that though Graves himself was in no way at fault, my friends in the Interior Building were nearer the truth than we any of us realized at the time.

Leaving them, I went on to see my friend Senator Johnson, who, as Maine's only Democratic Senator in years, had special influence at the White House, and told him what had happened. He had taken a warm interest in our project, not alone for its own sake but because also he was to come up for re-election the following fall and thought that the acceptance of our offer, bringing with it, as it would, recognition from the Federal Government of Maine's great coastal scenery, might help. He was properly indignant and, reaching across his desk, lifted his telephone and said:

"Give me the White House!"

Getting the President's secretary on the wire, he said:

"I want to see the President!"

The secretary — Mr. Tumulty, it was — replied that he was indeed sorry but that the President had every moment taken until he left the following afternoon for New York, where he was scheduled to deliver an address.

Senator Johnson, not well pleased, answered gruffly:

"I've *got* to see the President!" And rang off.

A few minutes later the telephone rang and Mr. Tumulty, speaking from the White House, told Senator Johnson that the President would see him at ten o'clock the next morning.

Mindful of what Mrs. Wilson had said of the President's doubt as to the legality of signing the Proclamation, I left Senator Johnson and went to Mr. Bond, secretary, as I have said, of the Public Lands Commission, and got him to supply me with full data on the Monuments Act, showing not only that what was asked was legal, but that ample precedents existed, some of them of the President's own making, while one, which he expressly quoted — the Muir Woods National Monument in California — reproduced almost exactly the conditions of our intended gift, though ours was on a greater scale.

With these papers in hand, I met Senator Johnson by appointment the next morning and accompanied him to the entrance of the Executive Chambers at the White House, where I waited while he had his interview with the President.

When he came out, he said:

"I had a good talk with the President! I don't believe he'll turn us down! I gave him your papers, showing the complete legality of what we ask and that his own use of the Act out west upon more than one occasion had established a clear precedent. Then I said to him, 'Mr. President, I don't want you to turn this down!' He wasn't born yesterday; he knew what I meant!"

Still the Proclamation did not come back, nor any word concerning it from the President to Secretary Lane. Then, soon after, I chanced to be dining alone one evening at the Metropolitan Club, where, at another table, was a group dining together, amongst whom were Governor Hamlin and Secretary McAdoo of the Treasury, who, separating from the others as they rose to go, came across to my table to greet me.

"Mr. Dorr," said Secretary McAdoo, "Governor Hamlin has been telling me what you are planning to create on the Maine coast and I want to tell you that I think it's splendid. If there is anything that I can do to help, I shall be glad to do it."

Then he went on to speak of a project for a central heating and power plant for the Government offices in Washington that his department, the Treasury, was at work upon, and that architects the country over were bitterly assailing. He would like, he said, to get my views on it. So it was arranged that he would call for me next morning at the Cosmos Club, where I was staying.

He came in his light, open roadster and we drove out through Potomac Park and along the projected mall of the L'Enfant plan. The power plant his engineers had planned was close beyond this on the edge of the Potomac, where it could be reached alike by rail and water, and it seemed to me then, as it still does, that no better, from all points of view, practical and artistic combined, could have been devised.

This I told him when we had looked it all over and then he turned to me and said:

"Now, what can I do for you?"

"Just one thing," I replied; "find out for me at the White House what the difficulty is that President Wilson does not sign our Proclamation." For Secretary McAdoo, as son-in-law of the President, was in the intimacy of the White House and might be able through this to ascertain what others perhaps could not.

The next day at noon I was in Governor Hamlin's office in the Treasury Building, directly opposite the White House, when Secretary McAdoo came in on his way back from a meeting of the Cabinet and said:

"I've come to report!"

His report was that Secretary Houston of the Department of Agriculture, who had at that time great influence with the President, had submitted a written memorandum in opposition to our plan.

I have never been able to this day to understand why Secretary Houston should have done this. It was distinctly an act of discourtesy to Secretary Lane in whose province — not his — the matter lay. Some element of the long antagonism between the two Departments must, I think, have been at the root of it. But at the moment I was less interested in the cause of it than in how it might be overcome.

Secretary McAdoo had told us that Secretary Houston had based his objections on the ground that he did not believe the National Monuments Act, under which we were proceeding, empowered the President to accept our tract and he had stated this in his memorandum, which was how President Wilson came to have that idea.

Governor Hamlin, who was a close neighbor of Secretary Houston at Washington and saw him intimately out of office hours, volunteered to take the matter up with him as one in which he himself took a personal interest and show him its legality.

Accordingly, I provided Governor Hamlin with the same material with which I had furnished Senator Johnson for his interview with the President; and, the thought occurring to me that Secretary Houston might shift his ground to the economic one, I added that if the question of the absence of funds came up, I had myself cared for these lands since I got them and that this I would continue to do, however long it might be, if the Government accepted, till Congress should see fit to grant us an appropriation.

Governor Hamlin had his talk with Secretary Houston and showed him, as he told me afterward, through proofs and precedents not to be disputed, the complete correctness of our procedure. As I had anticipated, the question of funds did come up and Governor Hamlin, prepared in advance, was ready to meet it. Secretary Houston then raised the objection that the Government could not accept gratuitous service. This, too, it had occurred to me he might do, and Governor Hamlin again was prepared to quote me, and did, to the effect that if the Government should approve the project I would take over charge of the Monument at the lowest salary paid at that time to anyone in Government service, a dollar a month. Accordingly, when the Monument was finally established I was formally appointed its Custodian at that salary. This I received at the end of two years' service from the Treasurer's office in a single check of twenty-four dollars which I presented to Mrs. Lane, the Secretary's wife, for her war-time hospital.

I had but slender hope, however, of Governor Hamlin's success in changing Secretary Houston's point of view; it was a case where prejudice might easily outweigh reason. So, playing my trump card, I had telegraphed that morning to President Eliot, to whom I knew Secretary Houston to be indebted for kindness shown him earlier in his academic career at Harvard as professor, telling him in detail what had happened and asking him, ignoring any knowledge of it, to write the Secretary in his own hand, not employing secretary or typist, inviting his cooperation in our endeavor, which he had much at heart himself as for the public good. It was now already late June and not knowing whether or not President Eliot had left Cambridge for his summer home at Northeast Harbor, I duplicated the telegram sending it to both addresses.

It caught him at Cambridge, I later learnt, just as he was about to leave for Northeast Harbor. He sat down at once and wrote to Secretary Houston a letter such as I suggested, dispatching it to me to read and mail in Washington. His letter began, with a dry humor which would be evident only to ourselves:

Dear Mr. Secretary:

I know this does not come within your province, but I cannot but feel that you will be interested to cooperate with Mr. Dorr and myself in what we believe to be so much for the public good. . . . . .

And he went on to outline, as though new to Secretary Houston, what we hoped and planned.

Taking copy of the letter, I mailed it in Washington. Three days after receiving it, Secretary Houston wrote President Wilson, in a letter which I later saw, as follows:

Dear Mr. President,

I have changed my view in regard to the proposed reservation on the coast of Maine and now think it highly desirable that you accept. . . . .

Very truly,

David F. Houston

Three days after he received this letter, President Wilson signed the Proclamation, on July 8th, 1916.

It had been a trying time; the weather in Washington had turned exceedingly hot, without let-up day or night, and everyone who could went off for weekends in the country or trips to the shore. But I had not dared to leave lest something unexpected should turn up. When all was over and I went to bid Senator Johnson good-bye, he said:

"Mr. Dorr, if you had not stuck nothing would have happened!"

And I felt that it had been well worth while.

Art Building, Bar Harbor, Me.

BUILDING OF ARTS, BAR HARBOR

On my return to Bar Harbor, following President Wilson's signing the Proclamation, a meeting was called by President Eliot to celebrate the event. It was held at the Building of Arts on a beautiful summer day, looking out as we sat there through the open doorways and the colonnaded porch across the green golf links lawn to the mountains now preserved in beauty and freedom to the public for all time to come, we felt, so long as the Nation should endure. It was a fitting climax to the long labor, the difficulties and anxieties the undertaking had involved, and upon it we rested, well content.

What was said at the meeting brought out so well the forward look, the vision that inspired us, then as now, that I quote it here in part, in spite of its repeating much that has been said before. The first speaker was President Eliot, who presided over the meeting.

PRESIDENT ELIOT

Ladies and Gentleman, Lovers of Mount Desert: We come together here to celebrate a very important step in a long progress—long as we look backward, and longer still as we look forward. Some of us have known this Island for many, many years. The first visit I made to it was just fifty years ago, and I have long been intimate with the Island and its surroundings. Most of us, I suppose, have lived here many years, or at least many summers; but the great event we celebrate today — the taking of nearly half the hills of the Island as a National Monument — has awakened a strong interest also in the Island on the part of single-season visitors, and those who come here for a few days only — or even for a single day. That is an important new fact; because the promoters of the present enterprise are looking forward to a large extension of the National Monument which will greatly add to the interest and attractiveness of this beautiful Atlantic Island at all seasons of the year. The old lovers of the Island expect to welcome many new lovers.

We who have long known the Island know that it is unique on the entire Atlantic coast of the United States, with nothing even to approach it in varied interest and beauty.

Now, the public spirited people who have got together by gift or purchase the lands which constitute today the National Monument have long been hard at work upon the matter — sometimes under discouragements; so they feel that today is a day for rejoicing and mutual congratulation. The labors of years have been brought to a cheerful and hopeful consummation. But these sentiments do not relate to their own experiences and their own happiness alone. One of the greatest satisfactions in doing any sound work for an institution, a town, or a city, or for the Nation is that good work done for the public lasts, endures through generations; and the little bit of work that any individual of the passing generation is enabled to do gains through association with such collective activities an immortality of its own. I have been accustomed to work for a University — in fact, I worked for one forty-nine years; but the greatest element of satisfaction in looking back on that work is the sense that what I was enabled to do, with the help of may others, is going to last — as good bricks built into a permanent structure. This is the great satisfaction of all the promoters of the enterprise we meet today to celebrate.

We hope to hear during the meeting something about the different stages of development of this enterprise. I hope we shall appreciate before we leave this hall what long-continued service a few men, and particularly one man, have rendered to this community through the work for the preservation of the Island's hills, woods, and water-supplies. I hope we are going to hear what needs to be done in the future of the same ends. For example, we must understand that other great hills of this Island need to be brought into reservation, to be held first by the Hancock County Trustees of Public Reservations or taken over directly by the United States. And then I hope we are going to hear from a very competent source of the new interests which are to be developed in the wild life of the Island, its trees, shrubs, mosses and flowers, and the animals that can thrive here on land or in the sea. This undertaking has a large forward look; and before this meeting closes, I think there will have been presented to us a picture of what we, the present enjoyers of the Island, can do for the benefit of coming generations.

The next speaker has been identified with the legal work involved in obtaining the great reservations which until a few days ago were in the hands of the Hancock County Trustees of Public Reservations. He knows the history of the enterprise; he also knows what the meaning of the undertaking has been in the minds of those who promoted it. I call on the Hon. L. B. Deasy:

HON. L. B. DEASY

Mr. Chairman: Not forgetting the many who have rendered valuable assistance, who have made generous donations of land or gifts of money to buy land, the chief credit for the establishment of this National Monument belongs to two men.

It owes its inception as a public reservation to the far-sightedness and public spirit of the distinguished chairman of this meeting.

It owes its successful accomplishment and ultimate transformation into a National Monument to the energy, the persistence, the unfailing tact, the consecrated altruism of George B. Dorr.

The movement for the creation of a great public reservation on Mt. Desert Island started in 1901, when, at the suggestion of Dr. Eliot the Hancock County Trustees of Public Reservations was organized under the general laws. Two years later, in 1903, the organization of this corporation was confirmed by a special Act of the Maine Legislature. The purposes of the Corporation as stated in this Act were to receive, hold, and improve for public use lands in Hancock County which by reason of historic interest, scenic beauty, or any other cause, were suitable for such an object.

It was not until 1908, however, eight years before the proclamation of the National Monument, that the Trustees received their first gift of land, the Bowl and Beehive tract on Newport Mountain, from Mrs. Charles D. Homans of Boston, a member of the earliest group of summer residents upon the Island. That same fall, through the initiative of Mr. Dorr and the gift of Mr. John S. Kennedy of New York, the summit of the Island — the old hotel tract upon Green Mountain, belonging to the heirs of Daniel Brewer — was acquired, to pass this summer into the Nation's keeping as the highest point upon our eastern coast.

Dry Mountain, Newport and Picket Mountains, Pemetic — the only one that still retains an Indian appellation — Jordan, Sargent, and the Bubbles, in whole or in at least their summit portions, followed steadily as the seasons passed, with the gorges and high-lying lakes that they include, till in 1914 an undivided tract, that seemed to Mr. Dorr and President Eliot worthy of offering to the Nation, had been secured.

Mr. Dorr, accordingly, went to Washington that spring and decided, on the strength of encouragement given him by the Secretary of the Interior, the Hon. Franklin K. Lane, to seek its acceptance by the Government under what is known as the Monuments Act, passed in 1906 under President Theodore Roosevelt, and widely since then made use of by the Government in western, still publicly-owned, portions of the country — this Act being one which authorizes the Administration, upon the recommendation of the Secretary of the Interior, to set aside by Presidential proclamation lands of "historic, pre-historic or scientific interest" as National Parks when previously owned by the Government or freely offered to it from a private source.

On Mr. Dorr's return, two further years were spent on study of the titles to the lands the Trustees had offered through Mr. Dorr, the extension of boundaries and securing of approaches to bring them up to the high standard that the Government requires.

Then, in the early spring of this year, Mr. Dorr again returned to Washington, taking with him all necessary deeds, and, supported by Secretary Lane, obtained the Federal Government's acceptance of the tract, the Proclamation creating the Monument being signed by President Wilson on July 8th.

The establishment of this Monument guarantees that it will be perpetually open for the use of the public, under due restrictions, not as a matter of sufferance but as a matter of right; it guarantees that it will be protected against devastation or commercial exploitation; that its animal, bird, and plant life shall be conserved — something that could not be accomplished under private or even corporate ownership.

The man who lives in the interior of the country has very little to remind him of the Federal Government under which he lives. But go with me upon the crest of any one of these hills and look seaward; upon every headland a light-house; upon every sunken ledge, a buoy or spindle. The safe channel along the whole coast is clearly marked; and when the fog curtain falls, the Nation does not forget its children upon the water, but guides them to safety by signals.

It is fitting that the Nation should be given this unique post of vantage, these mountains by the sea from which its most beneficent work may be observed. It is fitting it should hold them in trust for the public, because of the lessons they teach of ancient geologic history and Nature's ways; because of the exceptional variety and interest of the life they shelter, plant and animal; and because of their historic association with the early exploration of our coast and its attempted occupation by the French.

For these, alike, and other reasons of which I have no need to speak, so familiar are they to all, we do well to celebrate this occasion.

PRESIDENT ELIOT

Before I call on the next speaker, I venture to correct one statement in the otherwise entirely accurate remarks of Mr. Deasy. He attributed to me the early conception of what might be done here for the developing of a noble public park, thereby securing to future generations this Island as a great recreational resort. He did me more than justice. The conception in my mind was derived from my son, Charles Eliot, the landscape architect, who died in 1897. Moreover, the conception of our Hancock County Board of Trustees of Public Reservations was taken from the Massachusetts Board of Trustees of Public Reservations which my son not only conceived, but carried into execution. So it is to my son, and not to me, that the credit for the conception belongs.

I have, however, had a continuous function with regard to the work of the Hancock County Trustees of Public Reservations, of which I have been President. This function has been one of consultation, advice, encouragement, and now and then incitement; but this advice, this encouragement has been addressed to just one person, Mr. George B. Dorr, the principal worker in the enterprise, one great step in which we are now celebrating. I hope Mr. Dorr will say a few words to you not only on the nature of the enterprise itself, but on the future work which ought to be done for it; because he is not only a man of persistent enthusiasm and devotion to whatever he undertakes for the public good, but also a man of wise and far-reaching vision. I present to you Mr. George B. Dorr.

GEORGE B. DORR

Mr. Chairman:

My thoughts turn forward, rather, to the great opportunity that springs from what is now achieved, than back toward the past, save for the memory of those I would were here to be glad with us at this first stage attained. It is an opportunity of singular interest, so to develop and preserve the wild charm and beauty of this unique spot on our Atlantic coast that future generations may rejoice in it yet more than we.

But I trust it will be recognized that what we have now achieved is a beginning only and that our needs are many. We have entered on an important work; we have succeeded until the Nation itself has taken cognizance of it and joined with us for its advancement; let us not stop short of its fulfilment in essential points. We need more land, much more, that we may include all points of special interest and beauty in our tract and good approaches to it. The areas now adjoining it that are fertile in wild life — exceptional forest tracts, wild orchid meadows and natural wild-flower areas of other type, the pools haunted by water-loving birds, and the deep, well-wooded and well-watered valleys that lie between the mountains — are necessary to include in order to make the Park what it should be, a sanctuary and protecting home for the whole region's plant and animal life, and for the birds that ask its hospitality upon their long migrations. Make it this, and naturalists will seek it from the whole world over, and from it other men will learn to cherish similarly wild life in other places.

The influence of such work travels far; and many, beholding it, will go hence as missionaries to extend it. We have a wonderful landscape, to deepen the impression, and, now that the Government has set its seal of high approval on it, wide publicity will be given to all that we accomplish.

By taking the opportunity given us by the richly varied topography of the Island, by its situation on the border between land and sea, by the magnificent beginning made, and the Government's co-operation, we can do something now whose influence will be widely felt. And here I wish to say a word which falls in singularly well with the thought of the far-reaching influence this work may have.

Charles Eliot, Dr. Eliot's elder son, was a landscape architect of rare ability and enthusiasm. Moved by a public spirit that he derived alike from his own nature and the home influences that helped to form him, he initiated in Massachusetts the system of public reservations on which our own was modeled. To him Mt. Desert owes that debt of leadership, while he, in turn, might never have been awakened to the value and importance of such work had it not been for the inspiration, the love of nature and the quickened consciousness of beauty drawn from boyhood summers passed upon it.

During the early summer, when I was at Washington working for our Park's establishment and was plunged for weeks together in its oppressive heat, it struck me what a splendid and useful thing it would be if we could provide down here, in a spot so full of biologic interest and unsolved biologic problems, so rich in various beauty and locked around by the cool northern sea, a summer home, however simple, for men of science working in the Government bureaus, in the museums and universities. They would come down to work, as Henry Chapman and Charles Sedgwick Minot used to do, on a fresh field of life, bird or plant or animal, and then go back invigorated, ready to do more valuable work the whole winter through in consequence of this climate boon and stimulating change.

This is one opportunity. Another, which is urgent, is to secure now, while it may be done, tracts of special biologic interest, irreplaceable if lost in private ownership or through destruction of their natural conditions.

No one who had not made the study of it which I have can realize how various and truly wonderful the opportunities are which the creation of this Park now opens, alike in wild life ways and splendid scenery. To lose by want of action now what will be so precious to the future, whether for the delight of men or as a means to study, would be no less than tragic.

I pray you, therefore, not to look on what has been accomplished as other than a first step attained upon a longer way, which should be followed only the more keenly for the national co-operation that has been secured, the national recognition won.

PRESIDENT ELIOT

You see, ladies and gentlemen, that this celebration of an important step in the progress of a large public work has inevitably brought in the mention of simple domestic loves, of transmitted affections and dispositions.

I want to read at this stage a letter which I received this morning from Professor Francis G. Peabody, who has now his summer residence at Northeast Harbor, but who used to live in Bar Harbor. All through his early married life he was a resident at Bar Harbor.

My dear President Eliot:

I am prevented by a cold from attending the meeting at Bar Harbor today, but wish to express my keen interest in its purpose.

To one who has tramped over these hills almost every summer for forty-six years, the assurance that this privilege is to be secured for all later generations is a peculiar happiness; and I trust that the obligation laid on residents along the western shore to guard their mountains and water-supplies may be as obvious and imperative as it has been to their neighbors at Bar Harbor and Seal Harbor.

May I add one personal reflection? Mr. and Mrs. Charles Dorr were, from my point of view, late comers to Bar Harbor, having settled there not more than forty years ago; but they were the first to discover the possibilities of the shore for landscape gardening, and to transform the wild beauty surrounding their hospitable home into a well-ordered and unspoiled park.

How happy it would now make these devoted parents to know that among the names to be forever associated with the unique loveliness of this Island was that of their beloved son!

Cordially yours,

Francis G. Peabody

Mr. Peabody has in this letter referred to the need of guarding other mountains — Brown Mountain, Robinson Mountain and Dog Mountain.

Mr. Dorr spoke to us of another development which ought to take place on this Island — the study of its wild life of all sorts, its trees, shrubs and flowers, marine animals and land animals. Such studies add greatly to the interest of such a place as Mount Desert, both for adults and for children.

In Mr. Dorr's work to secure these reservations on Mount Desert and put them in the hands of the Government, he has found need of advice from scientific experts in all branches of natural history. This occasion would have been incomplete unless we had been enabled to hear from one of these scientific experts. I present to you Dr. Alfred G. Mayer, Director of the Department of Marine Biology of the Carnegie Institution of Washington.

DR. ALFRED G. MAYER

Ladies and Gentlemen:

There is something essentially American in this gift to the Nation, American in the sense that it must ever remain stimulating and constructive in regard to the character of its recipients, never arresting as so often were the gifts of older times. Yet was it an English friend of our land, Smithson — a lover of freedom and a man of noble dreams — who first established this modern form of giving in our country, when he bequeathed to it in his will funds for the establishment of the Smithsonian Institution.

At first men feared the very breadth of possibility it opened; but a great and leading spirit, Joseph Henry, so shaped this possibility into definite achievement that today no other single agency for the advancement of science upon this continent has succeeded so largely in constructive work as the Smithsonian. How fortunate you are, then, in having similarly, as founders of this present enterprise, two other great and leading spirits — our famous and distinguished chairman, Charles W. Eliot, and his far-sighted associate in this project, George B. Dorr.

For it is a project that contemplates far more than its mere gift of land, important though that be.

To Natural Science this gift, carried to its completion according to the plans now made, should prove inestimable; and it is as a naturalist that I must look upon these beautiful forests with their soft green moss and clustering ferns, and on the old gray rocks that bear so rich a growth of lichens.

But it is a meeting ground not of floras only; both the Canadian and Appalachian faunas meet here too, and so rich in bird life is it that Mr. Henry Lane Eno, ornithologist of the new National Park, tells me he has noted more than 140 species of birds during his residence at Bar Harbor, a wonderful list for any single area. Fully a hundred of these are land birds, many of whom will soon become delightfully tame under the Nation's kindly and protecting care. The rest are wanderers along the coast and strangely interesting, often, in form and habit.

The scientific study of this region is singularly rich in interest in many fields, with its fascinating geologic history, its glacial scars upon the ancient rocks, its grand fjord, Somes Sound, its splendid sea-cut cliffs and deep ravines; while the forest, with its "murmuring pines and hemlocks," its golden autumn foliage and dark green spruces, its density and interesting forest floor, is to me in its wild state the most attractive in the world.

Alone among the nations we possess a coast line extending from the pine trees to the palms, from the gray and all but arctic waters of Maine to the sparkling blue sea of Florida's Gulf Stream.

Our Government has, strangely, never established a permanent laboratory north of Cape Cod for our fisheries' benefit, yet no richer or more promising field for biological work exists than that offered by these fruitful northern waters, nor a more desirable and practical station for such work than that offered by the tract of sheltered and deep-watered coast at Mount Desert now dedicated to the memory of Dr. S. Weir Mitchell.

How deeply we need more information respecting our fisheries is all too evident. Why was it that in 1911 our fishing fleet obtained not more than one quarter of its usual and expected catch of Cod? Think of the millions that might be saved, the loss and misery averted, could we but predict the fisheries catch as we now do the crops on land. In Norway, where the study of the practical problems of the sea has made more headway than with us, they are able even to predict in accurate measure the seasonal growth of trees along the coast, and to determine ahead the earliness or lateness of the spring by observing the temperature of the neighboring ocean waters. Similarly a relation has been discovered between the abundance of those floating plants, the diatoms, and the fluctuations of the herring in the North Sea.

Many a problem of vital import to our race awaits the solution of these ocean problems, and the science of marine biology, with all the advance that it has made, is yet but in its infancy.

Let us hope that the guiding spirit of this foundation, George B. Dorr, and his wise counsellor, Dr. Eliot, may be given opportunity to establish it safely upon this larger basis, now that its first and hardest stage has been completed, and to continue the undertaking in like spirit to the past till a priceless heritage be secured to future generations, in an enduring opportunity for important work in a locality so favorable.

PRESIDENT ELIOT

The address to which we have just listened contains so many points of interest, so much of science and suggestive thought, that we must all hope that we may be enabled to read it. It ought to be printed for wide circulation.

This congratulatory meeting is now ended. We part with rejoicing in our hearts at what has been accomplished, and I am sure also with strong hope that the good work will be vigorously carried forward.

———————

The Monument established, the next step was to secure some annual appropriation for maintenance and protection. Up to that time all national monuments grouped under the Interior Department, lying wholly in the west and generally in remote and little-visited regions, had been allotted annually, in a single appropriation, but $5,000. The first year following the establishment of the Sieur de Monts National Monument no share even in this allotment was granted it, the Government's fiscal year having already commenced when the Monument was established. The following year it received as its share but a scant $150, which I expended wholly on ranger service for wild life and bird protection.

But there was nothing that could be done about securing any adequate and permanent appropriation at that time, nor until the Government's new fiscal year should open, July first, 1917.

So I returned to Boston to pick up old threads again and spend the late fall and Christmas season in old familiar haunts. Then, with the coming of the new year, I went on to Washington where I found a new spirit in the air, with war upon its way and great history in the making. It was a wonderful time to be there, each day bringing its own interest and new events.

On the 22nd of January, the President, in a notable address before the Senate, to which I had the rare good fortune to listen, outlined the kind of peace between the belligerents to which, he felt, America could subscribe. But a great change had taken place in the situation of Germany on the Flanders front; the Czar's government had fallen and Russia was now out of the contest, and the German High Command, free to turn its whole strength into the Flanders battle, felt confident of winning, at least so far as to enable it to dictate the terms of future peace. The transport of supplies to France and England, however, must be stopped and in the submarine the Germans had an instrument they now sought to exploit to the full. As a result of this a new situation developed suddenly at Washington.

On January 31st, 1917, a communication from the German High Chancellory was handed the President by its ambassador, Count von Bernstoff, announcing a new policy adopted by the German High Command, withdrawing all concessions made by it previously in regard to the use of submarines on the high seas or elsewhere, in defiance and utter disregard to American interests and viewpoints and its traditional, historic claim to the freedom of the seas. The German High Command was to be sole arbiter in regard to sinkings, responsible to none but to itself.

Three days later, President Wilson summoned Congress in joint session to receive the note and take action on it. The President declared that he had done his utmost to preserve peace but the limits of endurance had been reached. Within an hour after the President ceased speaking, the German ambassador was handed his passport and the American ambassador at Berlin, Gerard, had been summoned home. The Rubicon had been crossed and there was to be no turning back.

Ambassador von Bernstoff received his passport most solemnly, Secretary of State Lansing reported, averring he had done all possible 'to prevent this.' From that moment on the whole atmosphere at Washington was tense with war.

Congress was again summoned on February 26th to act on a bill for the arming of merchant ships, which, passed overwhelmingly by the House, was held up in the Senate by a filibuster staged by a dozen Pacifist Senators from the west who took advantage of the Senate's constitutional right, shared in by all, to unlimited debate. But the action sought was taken none-the-less, the Attorney General ruling, when a ruling on the matter was requested by the President, that since he, the President, was the Nation's Commander-in-Chief it lay within his power to order done without Congressional assent.

On March 4th the President entered formally on his second term and a new Congress came into being, which was summoned by him to attend in special session on April 2nd to act upon America's entrance on the war. I was present as a visitor, going early to escape the crowd which later filled the galleries and overflowed in a great gathering outside. The President made a noble speech, a really great one, ending with the words: "We will not choose the path of submission."

On this, the climax and conclusion of his speech, Chief Justice White, who had been sitting beside him on the platform and who was himself an ex-Confederate soldier, rose to his feet and cheered, leading the applause — an applause which came in overwhelming volume, sweeping all before it. It marked the entrance of America on her new role as one of the great world powers whose voice would be heard thereafter, and listened to, the whole world over.

I was grateful for the chance which had brought me to Washington at this time and lingered on to drink in impressions and scenes that never, I felt, could come again in such force and power during the memory of living man. Then, thought of the work I had left behind returning, I invited Secretary Lane, who had never seen the lands of the Monument he had helped me so vitally to get accepted, to come down with his wife and get a rest, staying with me at Oldfarm. But he could not, he felt, get away till the situation should clear itself as to the demands this new development that had so suddenly arisen might make upon him and I left for Chicago to get in touch with the Board of Trustees of the University there, with whom, among others, President Eliot had been working since his retirement from Harvard and whom he felt might help in carrying out my Wild Gardens scheme.

Arriving there, I found a telegram waiting me from Secretary Lane, forwarded from Bar Harbor whither he had addressed it, telling me that he found they could come after all and would take the night train from Boston, bringing them to Bar Harbor the morning of August 23rd. Getting this, I had just time to catch the night express east, which would enable me to join them on the train at Portland and accompany them to Bar Harbor, the approach to which was still at that time by ferry across Frenchman Bay. I had telegraphed on ahead and all was ready to receive us at my Oldfarm home. Arrived, I made my plans for showing them all I could within the limits of their stay, and had guests to meet them, old friends along the shore.

Their visit was a great success. One day I took Secretary Lane with me up Cadillac Mountain, he riding, I on foot, for he had heart trouble that made it unwise for him to climb. The old road, none too good at best, was now nearly washed away and I was anxious, as I strode beside him, lest his horse should slip on the broad, bare sweeps of ice-planed granite our way lay over. But all went well and he was tremendously impressed by the great sweep of sea and land that opened out before him from that high summit of the Island, and lingered long to view it.

When the last day of their visit came, I asked the Secretary where he would best like to go and spend the morning, and he replied:

"I'd like to go again to your Spring. What you have done there, with its broad human appeal and recollection of old scenes abroad, interests me more than anything else that I have seen."

So to Sieur de Monts Spring we went and strolled about. Alone for a moment with Mrs. Lane, I said to her:

"There's something I want to talk over with your husband before you go," and started to tell what it was when he returned and asked:

"What are you two conspirators talking about?"

I answered: "I was telling Mrs. Lane that I had just got word from the Chief Clerk of your new National Park set-up at Washington instructing me, as Custodian, to submit my estimate for the Monument this coming year. Having had as yet no appropriation to deal with, I have never submitted an estimate before and have no precedent to guide me. So I want to take advantage of your presence here and ask you, now that you have seen the Monument, to tell me what to ask for."

He thought a moment, then said: "Fifty thousand dollars!"

The Chief Clerk of the new National Park Service had instructed me, in the letter I had received, that in making my estimate for the Monument I should not at most exceed thirteen hundred and fifty dollars; this I had thought wiser not to tell the Secretary, but let him decide the matter freely and without suggestion. So I simply replied:

"You, as Secretary of the Interior, are the titular head of the National Park Service. I will write back and say that you, having visited the Monument and seen our needs, have instructed me to ask for fifty thousand dollars." And so I did.

When Secretary Lane returned to Washington he held to his point in spite of remonstrance and the estimate he had set was entered.

It was already the beginning of winter that year when I returned to Washington. I went at once to call on Mrs. Lane, whom I found at tea. Interested for me in what she knew I had so much at heart, she said, without more ado:

"I'm afraid it's no use!"

Comprehending her meaning, I said: "What is no use — to ask for the full amount that Secretary Lane instructed me to ask for, or for anything at all?"

"For anything at all," she answered. "Dining out the other day I sat next to Mr. Sherley and took the opportunity to bring the matter up. He would not even listen to it, but said, 'With the Nation at war, nothing new can be considered!' "

Representative Swagar Sherley of Kentucky was the autocratic and all-powerful head of the House Appropriations Committee, there being as yet no Budget Committee to review and pass upon appropriations, which all originate with the House.

To me it seemed that the point of new and old was not well taken and that all, whether new or old, should be dealt with on their merits. Not to give up without at least a trial, I went the next morning to Secretary Lane and asked him to give me a letter to Chairman Sherley, requesting that an opportunity be given me to tell him of the Monument and its needs. Rather reluctantly, for it was not in accordance with customary procedure, he wrote the letter, dictating it while I waited. Then, as I was leaving the room with the letter in hand, he called me back and said that he had changed his mind and would write himself to Mr. Sherley, asking for the appropriation he had bade me enter. This he did, while again I waited, then said, handing me the letter to read:

"Now go off and get some other letters in support of mine — letters that will count!"

The next day I left to get these letters, obtaining in all about a dozen, from people who would, I knew, be listened to on Capitol Hill. These all were mailed, as they were written, directly to Chairman Sherley.

Finally, returning from Boston and stopping over in New York for a couple of days on my way to Washington, it occurred to me to get a letter, in climax to my gathering, from former President Theodore Roosevelt, then at his home in Oyster Bay, as I chanced to see in the morning paper.

My first thought was to telephone him, knowing him slightly in a friendly way, but the telephone company, when I sought to call him, had instructions, I found, not to give out the number of his telephone. I was at a loss, for I was leaving that night for Washington. Then it happened that, going out into the street, I rant across his sister, Mrs. Douglas Robinson, an old acquaintance of mine, and, stopping for a word, told her I had been trying to reach her brother by telephone, and why, but that I could not get his number from the company.

"I can give it to you, of course," she said, "but I can do better for you than that — I happen to know that he is lunching today with Mrs. Wolcott at the Colony Club. Invite yourself to lunch with her and see him there."

I knew Mrs. Wolcott, the widow of former Senator Wolcott of Colorado, and it chanced that it had come my way to do her a favor in Rome, when I was passing through some years before. So I did not hesitate to write and tell her that Mrs. Robinson had told me that her brother was to lunch with her that day and that, wishing to have a word with him, might I come in for a few moments after lunch to find him? And so it was arranged.

When I got to the Colony Club, at the hour she named, I found them, lunching in a private room, still at table and went in and sat with them while they finished luncheon and afterwards till Colonel Roosevelt rose to go, when, turning to me, he said, for he knew that I had come to see him:

"I am tied up today with engagements that I cannot break, but won't you come with me in my car and we will talk as we go?"

So off with him I went. When we had started he turned to me and said:

"Now, what can I do for you?"

I started to tell him of the work I had been doing at Bar Harbor, when he broke in with:

"Oh, I know about that — it's fine! What can I do to help?"

"Write me a letter," I said, "to Swagar Sherley, Chairman of the House Appropriations Committee, in support of Secretary Lane's request for an appropriation for our new National Monument. Recently set up as it is, it has as yet received none worth speaking of and Mr. Sherley says that he will not consider any appropriation at this time, with the Nation at war, that has not been previously granted."

"I'll do it," he said, "Write me a letter in reminder and mail it to me at Oyster Bay. But be sure to mark it so that it will reach me personally — you'd be astonished to see what a mail I get!"

So I went back to the University Club, where I was staying, wrote my letter of reminder and mailed it to him in a Government-franked envelope, which, as Custodian of the Monument, I now had the right to use, writing my name on the outside and placing on it, for good measure, a special delivery stamp.

That evening I dined with the Hon. George W. Wickersham, Attorney General under Taft and a friend of mine at Bar Harbor, who had himself already written a letter to Chairman Sherley for

me, then took the night train to Washington. There, before I left
the Union Station, I sent Colonel Roosevelt a telegram to his
home at Oyster Bay, telling him I had written as I had promised
and asking him not to overlook my letter.

A few days later I got a letter from his secretary saying that
Colonel Roosevelt had written Chairman Sherley and enclosing
me a copy of his letter, which I insert:

April 10, 1918.

My dear Mr. Sherley:

As a man who has been deeply interested for years in the
growth and development of our National Park system, I respect-
fully urge on your Committee favorable action on Secretary
Lane's request for adequate appropriation for the Sieur de Monts
National Monument on the coast of Maine. It is our one eastern
national park and gives for the first time to the crowded eastern
city population of the country the opportunity to share directly
and immediately in the benefits of our national park system.

Its striking ocean frontage makes it unlike any other that we
have, and I have watched with keen interest the work that has
led to its creation. Under right development it will furnish a
health-giving playground, greatly needed to multitudes of hard-
working men and women; it constitutes also a wild like sanctuary under national guardianship at a point where such a sanctuary is greatly needed.

Secretary Lane's request for adequate provision for this park
is in accordance with the broad national policy for the conservation and development of our home resources — a policy which
every year becomes of increasing consequence.

Faithfully yours,
(Signed) Theodore Roosevelt

Hon. Swagar Sherley,
Chairman, Committee of the House on Appropriations,
Washington, D. C.

A few days afterward I received from Colonel Roosevelt a copy of Chairman Sherley's reply, which follows:

Dear Colonel Roosevelt:

I have your letter about the National Monument on the coast of Maine. We cannot at this time, with the Nation at war, do what we would at another, but I think I can assure you that an appropriation will be made.

Truly yours,

Swagar Sherley

This was the first encouragement I had got in response to the letters I had gathered. When the Appropriations Committee bill came out, the amount of $10,000 was allotted to the Monument, which was precisely what I would myself have asked for, had the opportunity been given me, under the conditions of the times.

The announcement of the appropriation was accompanied by the statement, which made it doubly welcome to me, that it was granted because the tract was truly one of National Park character and should be made a National Park. This provided me with the opportunity I was seeking for my next and final step: the creation of a National Park.

For this Congressional action would be required and if it were to be obtained that session there was not time to lose. Two bills to this end, identical in character, were entered promptly at my request, made possible by the fact that no appropriation was asked for or would be required, the one by Senator Frederick Hale of Maine, the other by Representative John A. Peters, serving this first term at Washington and there, as previously in Maine, of the greatest help to me.

Senator Hale's bill, speeded by Senatorial courtesy, received the prompter action; and, sent over to the House, was taken up in replacement of his own by Representative Peters.

At that time, I planned to call the Park the Mount Desert National Park. But at the hearing held when its time came by the Public Lands Committee of the House — one of some size and wholly composed, as it chanced, of western men — someone asked what the name meant. Was it really a desert?

And I had to explain that in the old French meaning of the word, in Champlain's time, the word 'desert' meant uninhabited by man, wild but not devoid of life.

Then another asked, "Where is it?"

And I realized I had counted too much on the knowledge of our coast and Island the country over. This caused me to reflect. The name I had taken for the Monument, that of Sieur de Monts, I would have liked to use but had found it difficult of pronunciation for Americans not versed in French. So I took the matter up with Senator Hale, whose bill it still remained, and told him my experience, saying:

"It would be of interest to tie up the Park's creation, in naming it, with the great events of the period and the war in France."

"Then," said he, "the name to take is that of Lafayette."

That was a time when the whole east was taking the war in the spirit of a high crusade and Lafayette's name was foremost in men's thoughts. After consulting with President Eliot and Congressman Peters, that name was taken, and Lafayette National Park it became and remained for the next ten years.

The Public Lands Committee reported favorably on the bill and the problem now became one of getting it before the House for action, in that crowded period. The only chance at that late date was to put it on the Unanimous Consent Calendar, to which one afternoon a week was given up, and this was done. As the name implies, a single objection to a bill entered under this Calendar is sufficient to throw it out.

Accordingly, the bill entered, Representative Peters and I visited certain influential members of the House to gain in advance their support, ending by going, before the House convened, to see the Speaker, Frederick Gillette of Massachusetts, an old acquaintance of mine, to ask who, beyond those we had visited, he thought might raise objection.

He named three who might be counted on, he said, to object 'on principle.' So we went on to visit them. The first two we found friendly when we had explained the matter; the third,

Victor Berger, a Socialist from Milwaukee, would not declare himself. We rose to go but as we took our leave, he said to me:

"Don't go! I'd like to talk with you."

So I stayed on, interested, and he told me of an experience he had had not long before in his home district and the tyranny of the war party there in forcing subscriptions to the Government's loans, illustrating his account with an incident which frankly outraged me in the hearing.

This was an instance of a group of the war party there going to a farmer in Mr. Berger's district and telling him that they had set him down for a certain sum in Government War Loan subscription, a sum greater than he felt he could afford to pay; whereupon he was told that if he did not voluntarily subscribe the amount they had doomed him for, they would take his automobile, a new one, sell it and put the proceeds into the Loan — which, he still refusing, they did accordingly. This, he told me, was but a single instance of a number of such kind in his district. The consequence was that he, a Socialist of genuine public spirit, lost the election and another man of dangerous subversive character was elected for the coming session in his place.

The following day our bill came up on the Unanimous Consent Calender. Article after article was called and disposed of while I waited. Finally our bill was reached and read.

"Is there objection? One — two — three."

The Speaker's gavel came down. Our bill had passed and the way ahead lay open.

The bill now passed rapidly through the routine stages of its further progress until it reached the desk of the President of the Senate, whence, signed by him, it would in due course pass on to the Executive Chambers of the White House for President Wilson's signature. But there it halted; there seemed no need for haste. With these two signatures alone remaining to obtain, one of them at least, that of the President of the Senate, purely formal, our measure I thought could rest secure, and I returned to Boston, there to wait.

On my way I made a brief stay in New York and took the opportunity to go down and see my old friend Judge George L.

Ingraham, one of the earliest among our summer visitors at Bar Harbor, rich in experience and ever full of tales of days gone by. His rooms were high up in an office building at the corner of Wall Street and Broadway, its windows looking down on both. Suddenly, while we talked, the bells began to ring and a great noise arose outside. Going to the windows we looked down on a tumultuous scene. The streets were filled with a rapidly growing crowd of clerks and stenographers, office boys and all, pouring out in swarms from the tall buildings and surging up and down the street in noisy jubilation, while showers of torn paper came fluttering down from the windows on every side. It was the 'False Armistice' of November 8th, which preceded the real upon the 11th, but was by far the greater demonstration. It was an extraordinary spectacle, one never to be forgotten.

President Wilson sailed for Europe in December, full of high hope for the future, to discuss with leaders there the terms of peace. Until he should return there was nothing more that I could do in regard to our Park bill, so I stayed on in Boston and waited there among old friends till word of his return should come.

Abroad he had a great ovation from the people, the conquered and the conquering alike, who put faith in him to bring about a better world, a world of peace and friendly relation among nations. Could his high vision for peace but have been fulfilled, as then seemed possible, incalculable suffering and loss might have been averted.

Sailing for Boston on his return, where he arrived on the 24th of February, 1919, President Wilson delivered before a great audience there a speech upon the League of Nations. I left that night for Washington, whither he arrived two days later with plans made to sail again on March 5th to attend the tragic, fateful Versailles Conference.

There was no time to lose if I were to obtain his signature to our Park bill before he sailed. Going promptly to the rooms of the President of the Senate at the Capitol, I secured, through a friendly secretary, his signature to our bill, and along with it signature to another of like character changing the Grand Canyon

National Monument in Arizona into a National Park. In this, Director Mather of the National Park Service took, as I knew, great interest and I was glad of the opportunity to help.

Getting the President of the Senate's office to entrust the two bills to me as a special messenger to the Executive Chambers at the White House, I took them over personally and delivered them to the President's secretary to whom I explained our need for getting the President's signature that night. For it had occurred to me that morning that under the pressure at the White House caused by the President's brief return, our bill and the other that I had in charge might, though taken to the President's desk, still rest on it unsigned. To make myself sure that this did not happen, I had purchased two fountain pens of the best make and taken them, filled with ink, with me to the Executive Chambers, planning to ask the President's secretary to get the President to use the one and the other for our two bills. This I did, and then sat down and waited while the day grew into darkness and night came on.

At last the time came, when to my dismay I found that the bills still needed the endorsement of the Secretary of the Interior before the President could sign. But the new offices of the Interior Department were but a step away and by good fortune Secretary Lane, busy himself over the President's return, was working late. He was in conference and again I had to wait. But presently, his conference over, he came out and I caught him as he left for home, got his signature, and returned, the two bills in hand, to the Executive Chambers.

The President worked that first, and as it proved single, day at Washington — that of February 26th, 1919 — on his return from France late into the night. A friendly assistant secretary whom I had interested in our need, watching his opportunity, laid our bills before him, got his signature and started them on the way to record before I left. The task that I had set myself to do six years before was done.

BAR HARBOR AS SEEN FROM BAR ISLAND

BAR HARBOR AS SEEN FROM THE TOP OF MALDEN HILL

THE MEADOW IN THE GORGE

SCENE ON THE SCHOONER HEAD ROAD

GEORGE BUCKNAM DORR

ACADIA NATIONAL PARK
Its Growth and Development

George B. Dorr

Book II

FIRST PUBLISHED IN 1948

This little book is published by the trustees under the will of Mr. Dorr, in accordance with his known wish. It is a narrative which completes his *Acadia National Park — Its Origin and Background*, printed in 1942.

As this unique Park would never have come into being, in all probability, had it not been for the public-spirit, imagination and unshakable determination of Mr. Dorr, and as he was the sole depository of all the details of the story of the Park from the beginning, it is proper and important, as a matter of history, that the record thereof be preserved in printed form for the benefit of posterity.

Begun a dozen years previously and completed two weeks before he died, the story was regarded by Mr. Dorr as the necessary culmination of his work for the Park, which commenced with the beginning of the century and which not even his total blindness could halt till he called it finished.

ACADIA NATIONAL PARK
Its Growth and Development

In January, 1907, when the Maine State Legislature had just opened its biennial session, my friend and neighbor at Bar Harbor, Mr. John Stewart Kennedy of New York, wrote me, then at my winter home in Boston, that word had come to him that a charter had been applied for authorizing the building of a trolley line over our main driving road from Ellsworth to Bar Harbor, with a branch as well through Somesville to Southwest Harbor, giving the fishermen there direct connection with the railroad at Ellsworth. For the salt fish trade was still, as it had been from earliest days, the principal industry at Southwest Harbor.

To obtain such connection with Ellsworth, the fishing interests had combined with a group of speculators at Boston seeking to get control of a quick, popular approach to Bar Harbor for its still rapidly growing summer trade. Such a line would ruin completely our summer driving upon the Island, which had been so pleasant hitherto.

Mr. Kennedy asked me if I would join him and Mr. Clement B. Newbold of Philadelphia, in taking steps to prevent it if possible. He was ready to bear himself the major cost, could it be done. I wrote him that I would gladly do what I could in the matter, but that the isolation of the Island that had been so pleasant in the past could not be counted on to continue in the presence of the summer life that had sprung up so actively and recently upon it and that it seemed to me the only effective way to meet the situation permanently and satisfactorily would be to build, ourselves, an electric line from Ellsworth to Bar Harbor, with the necessary branch to Southwest Harbor, taking it along new lines down the Union River shore and thence, crossing the Narrows on its own bridge, through woods and marshlands on the Island, leaving untouched, save for a few inevitable crossings, our driving roads; such a line to have its tracks connected at Ellsworth with those of the railroad, so that no change there would be necessary either for passengers or freight headed for Bar Harbor.

Mr. Kennedy answered that, looking at the matter, as we needs must, from the practical side, he agreed with me, and added that he was prepared to furnish the major funds for such an enterprise if it proved practical; and he asked whether I could not arrange to run down from Boston and meet the petitioners at Mr. John A. Peters' house in Ellsworth to discuss the situation. It seemed to me vitally important that if any railroad line were to be brought in upon the Island the undertaking should be in our own hands if possible, and I willingly agreed to go.

The meeting duly arranged, I took the night train down from Boston. To breathe the morning air and stretch my legs, I got off the train at Bangor at dawn, not waiting to put on my overcoat. The Station Master coming by, swinging his lantern, I remarked:

"It's a cold day!"

"Thirty-eight," he answered, and went on his way. This was thirty-eight below zero, the coldest, as it chanced, that I had ever till then experienced. But the air was dry and putting my hands in my pockets I continued trotting up and down the platform till the train whistled in signal that it was about to go.

At Ellsworth, when I reached Mr. Peters' warm and comfortable house, it was still far below. Our meeting went off well. The fishing folk at Southwest Harbor agreed to withdraw their application for a charter on my pledging our intended corporation to a real study of the problem and, should it prove feasible, to build such a railroad as I have described, branching on the Island to Southwest Harbor and Bar Harbor. Without the support of the Southwest Harbor fishing interests, there would be no chance the Legislature would grant a charter to outside interests, not demanded by the people of the region. And there the matter rested till we should have made our survey and study.

That afternoon I sleighed on to Bar Harbor. My caretaker at Oldfarm, John Rich, came over to meet me with my own fast horse and light open sleigh, with a buffalo robe for warmth, and brought me back to the house where I am writing now, warm and comfortable, though the thermometer outside, tempered by the sea, was still 16 below.

The next morning I made arrangements for taking options simultaneously, before word of our undertaking should get about, on certain strategic points that we would need should the road be built. Chief of all, for the terminal at Bar Harbor and control of its surrounding, I chose — with an eye to the future should our undertaking fail — a considerable tract off Main Street that now forms the Athletic Field, and the land to its north where Park Street now runs but no street then existed. At Southwest Harbor, for the fishing industry, I secured Clark's Point, well placed alike for steamboat connection and the fishing fleet; together with land at Ellsworth for a new, much-needed station and direct rail connection with the Maine Central lines. This accomplished, I went back to Boston, returning in the spring to start survey upon the line.

During the whole following season, from spring to fall, two excellent surveying crews, under Mr. Baker's supervision, made a thorough study of the entire route from Ellsworth to Bar Harbor and the branch to Southwest Harbor, the road crossing the Narrows by its own separate bridge and avoiding to the utmost possible all crossing or paralleling of the Island's driving roads.

Except for the entrance to Bar Harbor from Hulls Cove we had no difficulty in laying out a way with nearly level grade, such as I desired, whose standby-charge for electric power would be less than one-half of one percent. But from Hulls Cove to Bar Harbor, the northward continuation of Cadillac Mountain, ending in high bluffs above the sea, compelled a long, expensive circuit and a high electric charge over the whole line would have rendered impossible economic operation.

The Southwest Harbor folk, who had followed the work with interest, were satisfied that we had done the best for them we could and were content. And so the matter ended, but not without leaving a thought behind with me which was to bear fruit later in connection with our yet undreamt-of National Park.

Two years later, at the convening of the biennial State Legislature, January, 1909, an attempt was made by a number of the permanent residents of Bar Harbor to obtain repeal of a law passed some years before, when motor cars were still but crude affairs, prohibiting all use of them upon the Island. Duly warned in advance, a committee of summer residents, anxious to maintain the prohibition, was formed which defeated it, but not without criticism afterward of the methods used, a liberal fund being raised and placed where — as was stated later in a famous New York railroad case — 'it would do most good.' But the automobile was advancing with giant strides the whole country over and a fresh attempt to get the law repealed was planned to be made by citizens of Bar Harbor before the next meeting of the State Legislature, in January, 1911; this time I knew it would be serious.

Prominent features of Bar Harbor in those days were the fine trotting horses owned by summer residents, who brought them from homes elsewhere, and the annual horse show staged at the race track under Champlain Mountain owned by Edward Morrell of Philadelphia but built some years before by Martin Roberts, an outstanding local sportsman, with a like thought in mind; while one of the chief industries of the town was that of owning horses, buckboards and cut-unders and driving summer residents and visitors about on all occasions, furnishing a good livelihood to many of the native people which they would lose in great measure were automobiles brought in. Could the change, which I already then foresaw would be in the end inevitable, be brought about gradually, it would be far better; and a thought of how this might possibly be done came to me, which went back for its inspiration to the electric railroad we had made such thorough survey for.

My thought was that of a special road, extending from near the Bridge, on the Island side, to Bar Harbor, the law prohibiting automobiles elsewhere on the Island being retained still in full force. This would enable motorists coming from a distance to reach Bar Harbor with their own cars, but once they were there would make it necessary for them to use horses to get about.

This thought I talked over with a number of my friends, both summer resident and other, and found them cordial to the idea and, sharing my feeling about the inevitability of the future coming of the motor car, anxious I should proceed with it. Nothing was done, however, to carry out this plan; but that fall an attack was made on me for promulgating such a scheme and seeking to disturb the Island's peaceful life.

Active in the attack was one Mr. Bass of Bangor, owner of the Bangor Daily Commercial, who wrote an editorial on the subject for his paper, much altering the actual facts and holding me up by name as head and front of the offense. But it was all, I felt, a tempest in a teapot and I continued with my survey until the work was done and could be laid aside.

But the motor car question itself could not be thus dealt with and as the summer drew on into autumn it became increasingly evident that it would be hard for the summer resident committee, which had taken the matter in hand, to control it. The chairman of that committee, C. Ledyard Blair — the head of a great New York private bank bearing the family name — called a meeting at his home in New York of Mount Desert summer residents which I went on from Boston to attend. The gathering was a large one, for the matter was one which had aroused great interest among the Island's summer residents. There were a few among those present who shared my view that whether the opening of the Island to automobiles was to be desired or not, it was sure to come, and that it would be wise to provide in advance for their introduction so that it would cause the least disorganization possible of the Island's summer life. But the majority were strongly antagonistic and would tolerate no compromise. They were ready, quoting General Grant's famous dictum, 'to fight it out on that line if it took all summer.'

I listened quietly till all had had their say, then, addressing the chairman, said: "Mr. Blair, when the question of opening the Island to automobiles first came up two years ago and your committee was formed to defeat it, it was able to do so, but not without the employment of a substantial fund whose raising and expenditure incurred no little criticism. Since then the use and development of the automobile has come on apace the country over and the difficulty of keeping them off the Island will be correspondingly greater. How do you propose to defeat it now?"

"Defeat it in any way we can," he answered. At this Mr. William Lee, a friend and neighbor of mine at Bar Harbor, was taken aback, and exclaimed:

"Oh, Mr. Blair, you don't mean that!"

"Yes, I do," returned Mr. Blair; "defeat it — defeat it any way we can!"

Following this the meeting broke up. I went back to Boston, then on to Bar Harbor, where I had matters of my own to attend to that kept me on till the end of December, when, a day or two before I left, Mr. Deasy, counsel for the automobile exclusion group, came to me and asked whether I would be willing to meet, with him, Mr. Bass, now the only member of their committee remaining within reach, and talk the situation over.

I replied that I felt Mr. Bass had behaved badly in the matter so far as I was concerned but that if he — Mr. Deasy — believed it in the public interest, I would do so. He said he did think so, and it was arranged accordingly that the day I returned to Boston which was the day as it chanced immediately preceding the opening of the State Legislature, he and I would take the afternoon train to Bangor and have our talk with Mr. Bass, when I, leaving him there, would go on myself to Boston by the midnight train.

Now, there was nothing too much for Mr. Bass to do to show me courtesy. He had a closed, two-horse hack, such as city people used, to meet us at the train and bring us to his house, where supper was waiting. Supper over, we sat down and they unfolded to me what they had in mind, which was no less than to obtain my permission to make use of my survey for the special road as a basis for their bill, which they now held to be their only chance for success in face of the strong local demand which had by this time sprung up for complete opening. They wished to know whether I would allow them to make use of it, and on what terms.

I told them they might have it, and have it freely. But I added I had attended recently a meeting on the subject at Mr. Blair's in

New York and that I did not believe there was one chance in a hundred of getting the committee members' consent to use it or make any compromise.

"They are in New York," said Mr. Bass; "we are here, and they must do what we think best."

"All right," I said. "But you had better lose no time in entering your bill before they change their minds."

So I returned to Boston but I learned afterward they drew up and sent off a long telegram, marked urgent, to Mr. Blair, chairman of the committee, telling what they planned. They got forthwith a most reluctant consent, upon which Mr. Deasy and Mr. Bass sat up into the small hours preparing their bill for the opening of the Legislature the next morning. It was fortunate for their purpose that they did, for before the following day had passed they got a second telegram from New York rescinding the permission. But they were able to reply that it was too late; their bill was entered.

The Legislative Hearing on the question of opening the Town of Bar Harbor to motor cars, which extended to include the entrance from the Bridge, was held before the Judiciary Committee in its large auditorium, with seats sloping down toward the front and a dais on which sat the committee — one of the largest and most important in the Legislature. The room was crowded, every seat taken, with others standing at the back, for the question had aroused great interest.

The Bar Harbor summer-resident committee, a number of whose members had come up for the hearing, was represented legally by Mr. Deasy; William Sherman, Town Clerk and stationer at Bar Harbor, and Representative to the Legislature, led the townsfolk seeking the repeal. He and Mr. Deasy, as representing their respective cohorts, both sat centrally opposite the Committee which was seated in a row with their chairman in the middle. Altogether, it was a notable gathering and impressive scene, showing forth alike the importance of the occasion and the dignity of the law.

Mr. Deasy, who had secured an initial advantage by using my survey to offer a constructive solution of the problem instead of waiting on the introduction of the townsfolks' bill and then opposing it, opened the hearing, presenting the case for his committee with telling force. He had got hold of a publication sold by Mr. Sherman at his stationery shop, which, published as a guide to Bar Harbor, bore his name. In it was stated that one of the chief assets of the town as a resort was its picturesque, exciting drive "skirting the edge of precipitous cliffs, descending into deep ravines, rising up to commanding heights with glorious views——————." From this Mr. Deasy read such portions as were suited to his purpose, and ended by asking:

"Now, Gentlemen, do you consider this a suitable place to open to these dangerous new contraptions?"

Mr. Sherman, a most excellent man and valuable citizen but of a naturally nervous and excitable temperament, was unable at this point to control his feelings and sprang to his feet, exclaiming to the Committee:

"Gentlemen, I protest!"

Mr. Deasy, breaking off his reading and looking down over his spectacles at Mr. Sherman, asked, with the book he had been reading from in hand:

"Mr. Sherman, is not this your writing?"

"No!" shouted Mr. Sherman.

"Why," continued Mr. Deasy, "it bears your name. Do you mean to say that you put your name to what you do not write?"

Here the chairman of the Committee interrupted to say, "Mr. Sherman, you are out of order; you will please resume your seat."

Mr. Sherman reluctantly sat down, while Mr. Deasy continued with his reading from the pamphlet, commenting on it to the Committee as he read. But this soon proved more than Mr. Sherman could endure and he rose again to speak in further protest, when the Chairman preemptorily ordered him to resume his seat — he would be given his opportunity later, he said, to present his side of the case.

When the Maine Legislature is in session, the Augusta House, but a short walk away from the Capitol, is filled with people having legislative business to transact, or interested in hearings. When our hearing was adjourned at noon for dinner, it so chanced that as those attending the meeting streamed back to the hotel I found myself on the sidewalk, narrowed by a recent fall of snow, alongside Mr. Sherman, still smarting from his treatment at the hearing. Addressing himself to me, and seeking sympathy, he spoke his mind, ending up by saying:

"I used to think Ed Clark the worst, but Deasy's seven times as bad!"

The committee Mr. Deasy represented won their case, but a limit of $25,000 was placed on the amount the Town could expend on the new road's construction; the rest, whatever it might be, would have to be raised by contribution. The amount the Town was authorized to expend was promptly voted by it at a special meeting called for the purpose, but what was necessary to be raised beyond failed to materialize.

The net result of it all was the postponement for two years of the opening to automobiles of the Town of Bar Harbor's road system, and of that of the rest of the Island, with the summer residential colonies of Seal Harbor, Asticou and Northeast Harbor, for two further years, till the spring of 1915, which gave time to make the readjustment without too great change or hardship to stablemen and horse-owners on the Island. Besides, by the time the roads were opened to them the motor cars themselves had become far better, with their early crudities largely overcome, and the wider range and swifter movement made them welcome to numbers of the summer residents who had originally opposed their coming.

Upon the opening to automobiles of all public roads in the Town of Mount Desert, Mr. John D. Rockefeller, Jr., a summer resident at Seal Harbor, conceived the idea of constructing, for his own and his neighbors' use, a system of horse-roads over his land where they could safely continue to ride and drive as they had down upon the public roads before, but found himself blocked in doing so at the upper end of Little Long Pond by the need of crossing lands already then belonging to the Trustees of Public Reservations.

He asked the Trustees, accordingly, if they would sell him this land at the head of the lake that he might build his road across it. To take action on this, the Trustees' executive committee, with President Eliot in the chair, met at Seal Harbor and after due consideration declined to sell, stating that the land having been committed to them as a public trust they did not feel it lay within their power to return it to private ownership.

Mr. Rockefeller, not himself a member of the Trustees, then asked — through his representative at the meeting — if they would grant him the right to build a road across this land, leaving it open to the public for use with horses but with permanent restriction against the use of motor cars upon it. This, also, the Trustees declined to do since it would place a permanent easement on lands which had already at that time been offered to the Federal Government for a National Monument. But, to meet Mr. Rockefeller as far as possible in his purpose, which was of a public nature, they offered a counter proposition: That if he wished to build the road and take his chance with the Government, should it pass into its ownership, of restriction to horse use, he might do so. This offer he accepted.

Two years afterward, in the early summer of 1917, when the Hon. Franklin K. Lane, Secretary of the Interior, and Mrs. Lane came to stay with me at Oldfarm and visit the new Monument, for whose establishment by the President the year before he had drawn up the proclamation, Mr. Rockefeller asked me to submit to the Secretary a map on which he had outlined plans for an extended horse-road system, laid out in part over his own land but in part also on land which now belonged to the United States, and ascertain if he would give him permission to construct, at his own expense, the system indicated, for use with horses. I did better, for I arranged for Mr. Rockefeller's taking up the matter himself with Secretary Lane, inviting him to lunch at Seal Harbor and driving him out afterwards to see what he proposed. This was done and the Secretary gave him, personally, the permission asked.

Mr. Rockefeller proceeded to build these roads, taking his time about it, till all were finished save one, a unit in the system circling around the Amphitheatre Valley between the two branches into which Jordan Mountain divides, Cedar Swamp and Lower Jordan Mountains, and continuing on around the latter's southern end.

With construction just commencing on this, Mr. Rockefeller motored over from Seal Harbor one June morning in 1920 to

show me a letter he had received from Mr. George Wharton
Pepper of Philadelphia, a leading summer resident at Northeast
Harbor, which began by commending the roads that Mr.
Rockefeller had built and thanking him for the pleasure they had
given, but ended with requesting him to build no more. At this
Mr. Rockefeller was much perturbed, but said, after I had read the
letter, that if it should prove that Mr. Pepper's attitude was
widely shared among his friends and neighbors at Northeast
Harbor he would not wish, even though authorized by the Secre-
tary, to continue his construction.

To ascertain the feeling among the summer residents in that
section, Mr. Lincoln Cromwell of New York, president of the
Northeast Harbor Village Improvement Association, offered to
call a meeting of the Association for a frank discussion and a vote
upon it. Pending this, a group of a dozen or more met at Mr.
Cromwell's house to talk the matter over informally; and I was
asked, as now the representative of the Government, to attend.

Mr. Pepper was among those present and answering some
remark of his concerning the disfigurement of such roads, I took
issue with him, saying that rightly planned and carried out roads
of such character need cause no such disfigurement. In this
connection, I spoke of the beauty and pleasantness of a bicycle
path of wood-road character which I had built myself twenty-
odd years before on our own land beneath Champlain Mountain, where, circling a peat-filled, glacial pool, it took its way
through primeval woods of birch and hemlock; and, describing
the scene in autumn, I quoted some lines from Milton that came
to me as I spoke:

"Thick as autumnal leaves that strow the brooks
In Vallombrosa, where th' Etrurian shades
High over-arch'd imbower."

A few days later, I got a letter from Mr. Pepper in which,
referring to this, he said:

"When you quoted Milton, I knew my cause was lost."

But lost it was not, for as the result of Mr. Pepper's opposition, in which others joined, Mr. Rockefeller ceased construction.

Not wishing Mr. Rockefeller to lose his interest in the Park's development and needing, besides, to get some way of simple, wood-road character that would enable our rangers to pass readily between the northern and southern sides of our mountain range, for wild life and woods protection if nothing more, I told him of my need and that I would welcome the building of such a road along the western side of Jordan Pond to connection with existing trails below the Bubbles, looking down on Eagle Lake.

The suggestion interested him and he studied its possibilities that whole summer through with his surveyor. The result was an offer the following spring, that of 1921, to construct not only the road I had proposed but a whole connecting system beyond over the northern slopes of Sargent Mountain and on to connect, at its western end, with the horse-road system he had already built under the authority given him by Secretary Lane; and with this, in compensation as it were to the motorists who were now coming to the Island in ever-increasing numbers, an offer to contribute $150,000 for the construction of a Park motor road, the first it would have, from Great Pond Hill upon the Eagle Lake-Somesville road and along the sides of Cadillac and Pemetic mountains to connection with the Town road to Jordan Pond from Seal Harbor.

These offers, of motor road and horse road, were intended by Mr. Rockefeller to be regarded as a unit, to be accepted or declined as such, and I forwarded them to the Service at Washington with recommendation that they be accepted.

It was now the fall of 1921. I spent the winter and early spring over Park work in Washington and when I returned to Bar Harbor in June, 1922, I brought with me the Director of the National Park Service, the Hon. Stephen T. Mather, and his recently acquired assistant, Mr. Arno B. Cammerer. Mr. Mather came for a much-needed rest and change of scene from his work at Washington, not to study Mr. Rockefeller's plan, as he expressly stated, and stayed but a few days. Then Mr. Cammerer settled down to a study on the ground of Mr. Rockefeller's offer and presently, sitting on my porch at Oldfarm, dictated to my Park secretary a full report upon the roads proposed, ending with recommendation to the Washington office that they be accepted, which, accordingly, was done.

Work was begun on the horse roads, first, under Mr. Rockefeller's personal direction, for in these especially he took great interest, and then, in the fall of 1923, I started work on the motor road to Jordan Pond, commencing at the Bar Harbor end, on Great Pond Hill. No contract being let, the work proceeded under my own direction.

Here the way lay mainly over bare, glaciated rock and the work along the initial portion of the way, with no soil to freeze, could go on equally in winter and, once started, proceeded without delay. I then went off to Boston to spend the Christmas season among old friends.

Returning to Bar Harbor the beginning of the New Year I received in my morning's mail a letter from Mr. Cammerer saying that he wrote informally to tell me that, owing to an attack upon the road, made by Senator Pepper, I would receive shortly formal direction from the Secretary of the Interior, Hubert Work, to cease all road construction, pending an investigation. Mr. Cammerer added that this could cause no interruption to my work since none of such character could be underway, he knew, at Bar Harbor in that winter season.

In reply, I telegraphed immediately to Mr. Cammerer that I had received his letter and would strictly follow the Secretary's instruction when it came, but that I thought he, in issuing it, should realize that, far from having no men at work, I had a picked crew promised a winter's job and that if they were now turned off in winter's midst no power on earth could prevent it, with the names involved, from being a front-page item in leading newspapers the country over.

The next morning I got a telegram in answer instructing me, in the Secretary's name, to continue the work that I was doing but requesting me to come to Washington for a conference as soon as I could.

What had happened I learned immediately after by a private letter from my friend at Washington, Robert Sterling Yard, Executive Secretary of the National Parks Association, who wrote that the recently appointed chairman of the Path Committee of the Bar Harbor Village Improvement Association had come to him and asked for an appointment the following day to discuss

THE OCEAN DRIVE

A SCENIC VIEW ON THE OCEAN DRIVE

the road situation in our National Park; and that, soon after, Senator George Wharton Pepper, as he had now become by an ad interim appointment to fill out the unexpired term of Senator Boies Penrose of Philadelphia, who had recently died, rang up and said that he wished to come with Mr. Peabody to take part in the discussion. Coming, Mr. Yard said, he at once took charge of the meeting, bitterly attacked the work Mr. Rockefeller had done within the Park for horse-road construction, authorized by Secretary Lane, and threatened to take the whole matter up on the floor of the Senate. There he would speak under privilege; no opportunity would exist to check what he might say.

This, Mr. Yard wrote me, he had urged him not to do — if indeed he really had intended it — but, instead, to take the matter up directly with the Secretary of the Interior, Dr. Hubert Work of Colorado, in whose province it belonged; and appointment accordingly was made with the Secretary for a meeting at his office the following day, which Mr. Yard attended, when the Secretary, duly sympathizing with Senator Pepper on the destruction of the forest he described, ordered all work stopped until he could make investigation.

When I reached Washington, some ten days later, Secretary Work, placed in a difficult position between the facts as I stated them and his desire to meet the wishes of the Senator, who had come in with high prestige as a lawyer, announced that before deciding he would hold a hearing on the matter. This I arranged to have postponed as long as I could, which was the 24th of March — the opening of spring — that I might have time to organize our defense.

The date of the hearing settled, I returned to Bar Harbor and at once set out to organize the State in support of Mr. Rockefeller's proffered motor road, the first of any kind the Park would have, and, essential as entrance also, the road up Cadillac Mountain which I had had in mind from the beginning. I found no difficulty in obtaining support; the whole State was with us and when the hearing came I was on hand with a strong, representative delegation. The Governor and State Forestry Service, the political organizations and the Universities, all were represented, and a number of leading summer residents besides were present.

It so chanced that it was a Presidential Election year. President Coolidge was running for his second term and the Republican campaign was to open that summer in Maine. Senator Pepper, a distinguished jurist but newcomer in the political field, wanted to make the 'keynote' speech but in Maine they said that if he were to oppose the State's resort development interests, he would not be welcome as a speaker.

On my way to attend the hearing I stopped over for a day in New York to tell Mr. Rockefeller, who till then knew nothing of it, what had been going on and of the hearing to be held in Washington the following day. He felt, as I equally, about it, that to take the matter up on the Senate floor, where no opportunity for answer would exist, would be most unfair. That danger now seemed obviated, but since we had no knowledge of what might be said at the hearing, he took the precaution of sending his own lawyer to be present, unannounced, and take notes in case any statement calling for action should be made.

When Secretary Work opened the hearing at Washington the following morning the room was largely filled with the delegation I had brought on from Maine and others interested with us. The Director of the National Park Service, the Hon. Stephen T. Mather, not knowing how the affair might turn nor interested in it personally, had prudently gone west, the Service being represented at the hearing by his assistant, Mr. Cammerer, who, attending as a listener only, took no active part.

For the Park, the case was ably conducted by our Representative to Congress, Hon. John E. Nelson of Augusta, who called on one and another of the delegation to present their views, making, combined, a strong, clear statement of Maine's attitude in the matter.

Then Senator Pepper arose, and, recognizing, apparently, the representative character of the delegation and its friendly attitude toward my work, began with a most courteous reference to it and to myself, and said no word along the line of attack that Mr. Yard had reported him as mentioning in his office.

He was followed in due course by Mr. Peabody, chairman of the Path Committee of the B. H. VIA who, as it chanced, centered his attack on the work done by Mr. Rockefeller in the construction of his horse-road system around the basin of Upper Hadlock Pond where two major bridges had been built. Letting him say his say on this, I waited till he was done, then simply said that there was evidently some misapprehension in Mr. Peabody's mind concerning the work Mr. Rockefeller had done around the basin of Hadlock Pond for none of that area lay within the Park, but all was private property, owned by Mr. Rockefeller and lay wholly outside the hearing's scope.

The hearing at an end, Secretary Work announced diplomatically that he would postpone decision till the following summer when he would make opportunity to go to Bar Harbor and look the work over for himself, directing that in the meantime all construction then entered on should continue.

The next August, having occasion to visit President Coolidge in his Massachusetts home, he motored on to Bar Harbor, where I provided for his being entertained by Mrs. Henry F. Dimock of Washington, a famous hostess, who gave a dinner for him that same evening and turned him over to me in the morning to go out and look at Mr. Rockefeller's work. But, taking him over to Jordan Pond, where I had horse and carriage ready, I found he had no desire to leave his comfortable car for any horse-drawn vehicle; his interests were political and Nature entered into them but little. He left for Washington that afternoon and work continued as before. But no new roads in the Park were to be commenced without the Secretary's approval.

In securing the lands necessary to protection of the Eagle Lake Water supply, I had obtained for the Water Company and placed with the Trustees of Public Reservations the western, as well as the mountainous eastern and southern watersheds of the lake, but none of these western lands had yet been added to the Park; I had thought it wiser to retain them for the moment in the hands of the Trustees. These lands, Mr. Rockefeller, in carrying his horse-road construction round the northern face of Sargent Mountain, had now reached and entered on; and unless opportunity could be found for the extension of his horse-road system northward, his road construction and the acquisition of new lands which brought with it must cease.

As far as to the Bar Harbor-Somesville road at the foot of Eagle Lake, the way lay clear, but beyond this further progress was barred by the Town highway and unless means could be found for crossing it without exposing the horse-roads to entrance by motor cars. This difficulty, I thought, could be overcome by lengthening the grade of the Somesville Road, where it rose steeply onto McFarland's Hill, thus providing opportunity for an underpass for driving road connection, while benefitting the Town at the same time by easing the grade on one of the steepest hills in it whole system, impossible at times in winter. This I suggested to Mr. Rockefeller and, the consent of the Water Company, Trustees and Town obtained, he built the underpass and entered upon new territory which brought him finally to the Bluffs over Frenchmans Bay, where, through various gifts, I had already secured and placed with the Trustees of Public Reservations lands of striking interest and beauty, some hundred of acres in extent which Mr. Rockefeller included in his development, giving his horse-road system — extending now unbrokenly from shore to shore — a magnificent northern termination.

No sooner had Mr. Rockefeller started work on this new development than Mr. Harold Peabody wrote indignantly to Secretary Work that in spite of his instructions to the contrary a new road was being built along the western side of Eagle Lake. This letter the Secretary sent to the National Park Service with a demand for explanation and the Service sent the letter on in turn to me, when I replied that the road in question lay quite

"ROCKEFELLER ROAD" NEAR EAGLE LAKE

outside the Park domain, neither the Government nor the Secretary having jurisdiction over it.

Further correspondence followed between Mr. Peabody and the Secretary of which copies were forwarded me by the Service. There, so far as the Government was concerned, the matter ended, Mr. Rockefeller proceeding with his work.

To tell now the story of our Schoodic acquisition: Schoodic Peninsula frames the entrance to Frenchmans Bay upon the eastern side as the cliffed shore of Mount Desert from Great Head to Compass Harbor does upon the western, with Egg Rock and its long line of surf-swept ledge between, fronting the open sea.

Schoodic Peninsula, extending from Frazier Creek to the wild, storm-beaten point in which it ends, is the furthest rock-built projection of the mainland into the Atlantic Ocean of any on our eastern coast. Back from its end by half a mile the promontory rises into a magnificent head, precipitously cut by the breaking waves of a stormy sea during the glacial period when the coast stood at a lower level in relation to the ocean.

The view from this Head is one of the greatest in the world in its own coastal type, unbroken to the south in its grand seaward sweep and stretching eastward to the Bay of Fundy, whence down the long reach of water one sees the rising sun; and westward, across the broad entrance to Frenchmans Bay, to the sunset and the Mount Desert Mountains.

Opposite the base of the Peninsula lies Winter Harbor, one of the best and safest ice-free harbors on the coast, enclosed upon its western side against Frenchmans Bay by Grindstone Neck, the home of a considerable summer colony.

One evening in late September, 1922, taking supper with friends at the Jordan Pond House, I chanced to sit next a neighbor of mine on the Bar Harbor shore, Mrs. Warner M. Leeds, the widow, before her marriage to Mr. Leeds, of Mr. John G. Moore, whose second and much younger wife she was, a friend of his daughters by his first marriage, with whom she used to come and stay. To Mr. Moore was largely due the building up of Winter Harbor as a coast resort. A native of the town of Steuben on the nearby coast, he had gone to New York as a lad to make his fortune, had risen by successive steps to found one of the leading brokerage houses in the city and, wealth achieved, returned and interested himself in the development of his native regions, organizing the 'Shore Line' railroad from Ellsworth to Eastport and the Canadian boundary, and taking a leading part in the building up of a resort at Winter Harbor comparable to those on Mount Desert Island. With this last aim in view, he acquired a number of sites on Grindstone Neck for additional summer home development and Schoodic Peninsula for a wild parkland to hold in connection with it. Then, in the midst of his planning and activities, he died.

The home Mr. Moore built for himself in a commanding situation upon Grindstone Neck was sold to Mr. Frank B. Noyes of Washington, president of the Associated Press, and his interests in the real estate association at Grindstone Neck were taken over by a wealthy fellow colonist, interested like himself in the resort's development. But the wild parkland of Schoodic Peninsula, which Mr. Moore had retained in his own possession, passed into his estate, left in equal portions to his widow and his two daughters.

As we talked together that night at supper, concerning, among other things, the work I was doing in gathering lands on Mount Desert Island for public reservation, Mrs. Leeds asked if I would not like to have her interest, a third, in Schoodic Peninsula. I knew the tract well, having sailed over again and again in early days to climb the Head for its great view, and I said at once that I would assuredly be glad to have it.

The following day, crossing the bay in the Leeds yacht, we got a team and drove to Schoodic Head over the old horse-road built some twenty years before by Mr. Moore, taking along a photographer whom I had at that time in my employ for securing pictures in the Park, who took a photograph of Mrs. Leeds as she stood upon the Head.

Immediately after, Mrs. Leeds left to go abroad, planning to meet in England Mr. Moore's two daughters and ascertain if they would not like to share in giving the Schoodic tract for public reservation in their father's memory. One of these daughters had married, earlier, a young English diplomat, resident at the time in Washington, who had since become Lord Lee of Fareham. The other daughter, Miss Faith Moore, who had never married, dwelt nearby in England to be with her sister.

Before Mrs. Leeds had opportunity to take the matter up with Lady Lee and her sister, however, she had a breakdown and, returning to America, died soon after; and the interest in the Schoodic property she had offered me for our Public Reservations remained in her estate.

Mrs. Leeds had had no child by either marriage and to replace the loss they felt, she and Mr. Leeds had adopted two children, a boy and a girl. The boy died early; the girl, to whom they gave the name of Joy, became their heir. The property which came to Mrs. Leeds through her first marriage, to Mr. Moore, was considerable and passed on her death to her second husband and their adopted daughter, yet a child. Mr. Leeds was one of his wife's executors, the other being a New York lawyer who had been associated with Mr. Moore during his work at Winter Harbor. As executor, Mr. Leeds, naturally of a thrifty nature and with the adopted child's interest in mind, was reluctant to carry out his wife's intended gift of her one-third interest in the Schoodic parkland, but offered it instead for sale to the Trustees of Public Reservations. Failure to acquire this would have cost us the free gift of the remaining two-thirds interest I had by that time secured conditionally from Lady Lee and her sister in England.

This presented an unforeseen complication which needed patience and no slight amount of tactful handling to overcome, but which, with some yielding on non-essential points upon the Trustees' part, was finally straightened out and secured not only Schoodic Head, as Mrs. Leeds intended, but opportunity for the most powerful and sensitive overseas radio station on our Atlantic coast, which has now passed, through the Trustees' gift, into the hands of the National Government to maintain permanently, and is essential to its whole naval base, underseas and flying development in this greatest and most epoch-making of World Wars.

In 1924 opportunity presented itself for the acquisition of one of the most beautiful sites upon the coast, that on which Mrs. Charles D. Homans of Boston, an old friend of mine and my family's and of President Eliot, had built her home and spent her summers until she died.

I was most anxious to secure it for the Park and Mrs. Homans' executors, desirous that I should, made the way as easy for me as they legally could. I took the matter up with friends of mine, Mr. and Mrs. Herbert Satterlee, who had been her friends as well and neighbors on the Great Head shore, who generously responded; and President Eliot, interested no less than I, raised other funds, while I contributed myself what yet remained. The estate was purchased and given into the keeping of the Trustees of Public Reservations, pending transfer to the Government for the National Park when the way should open.

For this and the transfer of Schoodic, directly opposite, across the entrance to Frenchmans Bay, the opportunity came four years later by one of those unlooked-for chances which, taken as they present themselves, have created and are still creating Acadia National Park.

In the fall of 1928, word reached me from Washington that Congressman Cramton of Michigan, Chairman of the House Appropriations Committee for the Department of the Interior, had gone to Canada on a motor trip with his wife and might take in the Park on his way back if I got in touch with him. This I did at once, inviting them to come and stay with me as my guests on their back to Washington. They came and spent three days with me at Oldfarm, and it was an extraordinarily fruitful visit.

I told Representative Cramton of our Schoodic reservation awaiting the Government's acceptance and of my hope for its establishment as a National Monument.

"Why do you not include it in the Park?" he asked.

That, I told him, was what I had hoped at the start to do, but two obstacles had blocked my way: First, the name of the Park — and I told him of Lady Lee's and her sister's objection to the name of Lafayette; and second, an act of Congress would be necessary, since when the bill creating the Park was drawn I was able only to secure, looking to the future and the Park's increase, authority for the Secretary of the Interior to accept gifts of land lying on Mount Desert Island, and Schoodic lay upon the mainland.

"Is there any other name for the Park you would like as well?" he asked.

"Yes," I said, "the name of Lafayette was taken because of the strong war-time feeling at the time of the Park's creation; I have often since thought that Acadia, because of its old historical associations and descriptive character, would have been far better."

Then he said: "If you will get a bill drawn up and entered by your Congressman to change the name of the Park and extend the power of the Secretary to accept lands beyond the bounds of Mount Desert Island, on the neighboring mainland, I will place myself behind it and we will put it over."

I took Congressman Cramton also to the Homans House, showing him its wonderful view and appropriateness for the Park's possession, and told him of the difficulty I was encountering in getting it accepted because repairs to the house were needed and the Service was without funds for making them. And there I let the matter lie for his consideration.

As soon as Representative and Mrs. Cramton left, I motored over to Augusta to find our Congressman, the Hon. John E. Nelson, and together we drew up a bill. This bill it was agreed he introduce immediately on his return to Washington for the coming session. It called for changing the name of the Park to Acadia and extending the power of the Secretary to accept in his discretion offers of lands lying anywhere within the County of Hancock, in which Mount Desert Island and Schoodic both lie.

On his return to Washington, Congressman Cramton did not forget us. I received soon after a letter from Mr. Cammerer, Associate Director, saying that Congressman Cramton had informed him that if I would submit plans and estimates for the repairs and alterations of the Homans House, he would make provision for them in the Park appropriations for the coming year. Mr. Cammerer added that no funds were available for making these plans but he felt sure that of this I would be able to take care. The Interior Department Appropriations Bill, he added, was about to close and there was no time to lose.

I straightway did what he suggested, employing at my own charge a local architect and builder and with plans and estimates in hand took the first train for Washington.

There I found Mr. Cammerer too busy and preoccupied with other matters to go with me to Mr. Cramton's office. I asked if I had not, then, best go without him, to which he answered that it would be of no use — that Mr. Cramton, at work upon his bill, could scarce make time to see him himself when he last went over and quite certainly could not, at this late hour, find time for me. I waited on another day and it was still the same; so, taking the matter into my own hands, I went over on the third day in the late afternoon, when I thought the stress of his work would be over, to find Congressman Cramton in his office at the Capitol. He was alone with his secretary and delighted to see me. I showed him my plans and estimates for the Homans House and he said:

"You're just in time! Tomorrow my bill will close and in another day you would have been too late."

He then asked me to return the following noon and lunch with him and his committee at the House restaurant. I said:

"That means you would like to have your committee look me over."

He laughed and said:

"That's about the size of it!"

So the next day I returned for a very pleasant lunch and after it went over briefly, with him and his committee, my plans and estimates. They forthwith acted favorably upon them and entered them in the Bill, less than an hour before its closing.

And this is how, my difficulties over, Acadia National Park acquired at once its guest house and its name.

Mount Desert Island has but one stretch of frontage on the open sea, extending from Great Head, at the entrance to Frenchmans Bay, westward to Otter Cliffs. A beautiful sand beach with a fresh water lagoon behind it, where the deer come down to drink, separates Great Head from the rest of the shore — a rugged shore, built on granite with a reddish hue and backed by

THE LADDER TRAIL, BEEHIVE MOUNTAIN

the rocky heights of Gorham Mountain and the Beehive in which the long narrow ridge of Champlain Mountain ends toward the south. On these rocks the surf comes rolling in magnificently after storms at sea, dashing up in solid masses, then falling in great showers of spray. At their southwestern end these rocks project out superbly in massive granite cliffs, Otter Cliffs, beyond which the sea reenters in the long submerged cleft of Otter Creek. At the eastern end, Great Head and the Sand

Beach belong not to the Government but to Mr. and Mrs. Herbert L. Satterlee, who live there in a simple fashion according delightfully with the rare beauty of the setting, and leave the western portion of the beach open to visitors, a privilege precious above all to children.

In March, 1929, I was staying with my friend and fellow-citizen at Bar Harbor, Mr. Gist Blair, in the historic old Blair mansion on Pennsylvania Avenue, opposite the War and Navy Building, when he brought up to me the question of the future of this land, so important to preserve, uncommercialized and undisfigured, to the enjoyment of the future. It had come by inheritance to an old Bar Harbor family who now wished to sell it; it would be a tragedy should it pass into wrong hands. Mr. Blair took, at his own expense, a six months' option on it, hoping to raise the purchase price by subscription among the Bar Harbor summer residents, but nothing came of it. I did not regret it for I thought that if he failed, Mr. Rockefeller might step in and take it in continuation of an extensive shore frontage he had earlier acquired west of Otter Creek, and that if he did he would purchase also the bold projecting head of Otter Cliffs, separately held and equally in the market, and develop them all as a unit for the public benefit, turning them over ultimately to the National Park. And this is what did happen.

Early the following fall, Mr. Rockefeller drove over to see me and tell me of a plan he was at work upon for linking up Cadillac Mountain with these new lands upon the ocean front.

The next spring Mr. Rockefeller had two surveying crews in the field sent out by a leading New York engineering firm, who worked all summer In the fall, his plans completed, he made a formal offer to the Secretary of the Interior and the National Park Service to build a continuous Park motor road, connecting unbrokenly the Cadillac Mountain Road with the ocean-front, and at the same time two additional horse-roads which he had long had in view, in extension of his already constructed horse-road system. A map setting forth this offer was sent down from Washington to Acadia National Park for exhibition in its office.

No sooner had the plan been posted and announcement of it made than a storm broke loose yet more bitter, if possible, than that which had been provoked in 1924 by the building of the road contributed by Mr. Rockefeller to connect Bar Harbor through the mountains with the Seal Harbor Road to Jordan Pond and his horse-road system encircling Sargent Mountain which accompanied the offer.

VIEW FROM SARGENT MOUNTAIN

Letters by the score were sent to Washington and referred back to me to read and comment on. Some of the criticisms made were just and well taken; the majority showed only prejudice, lack of understanding and unwillingness to face the problem. The Secretary of the Interior gave little heed to them, however, and, supported by the National Park Service, accepted Mr. Rockefeller's offer.

Work was commenced by him the following spring on the Amphitheater Road begun twelve years before, from whose construction, in deference to the opposition of Mr. Pepper and his friends, he had withdrawn, but which he had since come to feel essential to his horse-road system.

Work was begun by him also on the reconstruction of the Ocean Drive, which the Town at its annual March meeting had turned over to the Park in support of Mr. Rockefeller's aim, but progress on it was delayed pending removal of the obstacles presented by conditions which accompanied Mr. Rockefeller's offer. The chief of these and the most difficult to satisfy was the removal of the Otter Cliffs Naval Radio Station to another site, a removal to which the naval authorities at Washington, Secretary Adams apart, raised strong objection.

The Otter Cliffs Radio Station, developed in the first instance in response to a war emergency need, had proved a wonderful receiving station — a station so excellent that it had been used exclusively during President Wilson's stay abroad for his communications with Washington. No site less favorable would be acceptable, in exchange, to the Navy Department, I knew, and there was but one location which I thought might equal it — the far seaward projection of Schoodic Peninsula, the Park's recent acquisition.

The matter was taken up with the Navy Department and in May Rear Admiral Philip Andrews, stationed at the Boston, Massachusetts, Navy Yard, in charge of the First Naval District, came down to look the situation over with me. Familiar with the coast, he declared at once that there was but a single situation on it which could equal, and might perhaps surpass, in favorable radio conditions the site at Otter Cliffs: Schoodic Peninsula, the only question being its adaptability to a radio station's need.

We visited the site together, Assistant Superintendent Benjamin L. Hadley and Park Engineer Walters G. Hill making up, with us, the party. Looking the situation over, the chief difficulty which presented itself was the lack of water for the station's need. The same difficulty had been met and overcome at Otter Cliffs by the drilling of artesian wells. The lay of the land at Schoodic gave equal promise and Mr. Hadley and Mr. Hill took charge of the search for water, employing an experienced local firm to drill, and after several trials water in abundance was found. Admiral Andrews returned to Boston Navy Yard and we wrote of his favorable report to Washington.

There seemed at that time nothing that need prevent the transfer to Schoodic, provided the Secretary of the Navy and his staff at Washington consented, while a strong argument in favor of the removal presented itself in the condition of the buildings at Otter Cliffs, built for the war-time need and not for permanence. Wherever the station might be located, new buildings would be required, and if at Schoodic the National Park Service would provide the funds.

In June, Horace M. Albright, former Field Director who had succeeded Mr. Mather as Director, following the latter's fatal illness the previous year, came down to look the situation over, bringing with him the Service's Chief Engineer, Oliver G. Taylor and Landscape Architect Charles E. Peterson.

We went at once to Schoodic to look over the proposed site. The endorsement of Admiral Andrews given and water found, the next matter was the construction of a road to reach the site. A preliminary survey for it had been made under the National Park Service's Landscape Division, which we now proceeded to review. The road, some miles in length, picturesquely skirted the rugged western shore of the Peninsula and approximate estimates of cost had been prepared, placing it at slightly less than $300,000.

This survey, with some slight alterations in the interest of beauty, was given tentative approval and a superb termination for the road in a round-turn and parking ground among the great rocks at the storm-swept tip of the Peninsula was added to it.

Director Albright, who had never visited Acadia National Park before, expressed his warm interest in it and desire to help. Then, the following day, he left, the Chief Engineer, Oliver G. Taylor, remaining to spend some weeks with us, making various surveys. Admiral Andrews had now retired and his place was taken by another admiral less familiar with our coast, and strenuous opposition to any removal of the radio station from Otter Cliffs developed at Washington, centered on the loneliness of the Schoodic site and the absence of good road connection.

The Secretary of the Navy himself, however, Charles Francis Adams, the younger, an old friend of mine in Boston, was well-disposed toward the project but, with all good will, could not go counter to the advice of his official staff.

An impasse followed which lasted through the summer and the National Park Service at Washington grew discouraged. This both I and those interested with me at Bar Harbor refused to become and when, in the early summer, I learned that three and a half million dollars had been added by Congress to four million already granted and allocated to road construction in the western parks, I telegraphed the Director, then gone again out west, asking him to set aside $200,000, if no more, for the road at Schoodic, important, even though the radio station plan should not go through, as a great coastal drive. I had no answer till the fall, when a brief word came that the entire amount — the new appropriation as well as the old — had been allotted to projects in the west.

Meanwhile, the time limit set by Mr. Rockefeller for fulfillment of his condition was drawing near; all other obstacles had been cleared away, but this, if it remained, would be fatal. A magnificent coastal drive, of inestimable value to the future, hung in the balance; to secure it we must act without delay.

Enlisting Judge Peters' help, I took the matter up through him with Senator Hale, now chairman of the Senate Naval Committee, alike influential with the Navy Department and interested in Maine affairs, and directly with our Representative to Congress, Hon. John E. Nelson of Augusta.

Senator Hale at once took a hand and got the Navy Department to send down again Captain Hooper, chief of the opposing experts, with instructions not to return without coming to some settlement of the problem.

Congressman Nelson, going to the navy Department's rooms, sought Captain Hooper out and had a frank talk with him. It must have been a truly frank talk, for Captain Hooper said:

"You insult me!"

"I mean to," said Congressman Nelson.

But they parted friends.

Captain Hooper came and brought with him a younger officer from the Boston Navy Yard, who proved a helpful ally in our cause.

I had, however, come to the conviction that no progress would be made so long as we had to rely solely upon the Navy Department experts testifying upon matters that were a mystery to laymen. I spoke of this to David O. Rodick of Deasy, Lynam, Rodick and Rodick of Bar Harbor, leading attorneys, and he reached out for his telephone and asked for the radio expert division of the great Jefferson Physical Laboratory at Harvard.

Obtaining connection with its chief he asked if he could not come down for consultation on an important radio communication matter, outlining to him what it was. The chief, a man whose authority would be respected in all radio communication circles the country over, replied that he could not at the moment leave but that he had two younger assistants no less expert than he, either of whom could come. Mr. Rodick asked what the cost would be and was told $500.

"Send one of them along," Mr. Rodick said.

Deciding to split the fee, both came and went over the matter thoroughly in advance of the Government experts' coming.

In the course of their investigation into the receptivity of the Schoodic site, the men from Harvard put in twenty-four hours vigil in a ranger cabin we had built nearby, erecting from it a temporary aerial, put up there to catch what the air might bring. During the night they intercepted one communication from Australia and another from Japan, the latter of which they thought might have come over the North Pole to reach them, besides catching a number of communications from ships at sea or those entering British or European ports. There could be no question, they said, as to the exceptional radio receptive fitness of the Schoodic site. Objection could center only on the relative isolation for its personnel.

Captain Hooper, when he reach Bar Harbor, was still determined to retain the Otter Cliffs site, though ready, with the promise of a new building, to shift, within certain bounds, the position of the station.

The day of his arrival was cold and rainy, with mists rolling in from the sea, but he kept the whole party out with him in the dripping woods at Otter Creek, exploring the terrain for an alternate site. In the afternoon, clothes dried and the inner man restored, we met again at the office of Mr. Harry Lynam, acting alike for the Government and for Mr. Rockefeller, and Captain Hooper made various proposals for changing the building — not the site. And he insisted that if Mr. Rockefeller only understood what he proposed, he would yield at once. Mr. Lynam arranged for him to talk direct with Mr. Rockefeller and the wire to New York was held open for half an hour; but it was all to no avail. Mr. Rockefeller would not yield an inch.

The next morning we met once more at Mr. Lynam's office. The day again was rainy and disagreeable. Captain Hooper announced that he had explored every possibility. No solution could be found, he said, and he was ready to return to Washington.

"Captain Hooper," I said, "you were sent down here from Secretary Adams' office with instruction not to return without coming to some agreement. You have done your best to retain a site at Otter Cliffs, without success. You have not been over to Schoodic."

"I went over that before," he said, "and reported adversely on it. It will not do."

"I know about your visit to Schoodic," I replied, "and the spirit in which you made it. You came determined in advance to turn the proposition down. Your report was biased and you made no fair investigation. You cannot return to Washington now, under the instructions you have received, without at least visiting the Schoodic site again."

And reluctantly he consented.

Mr. Walters G. Hill, our engineer who had helped on the road survey and the search for water, offered to take Captain Hooper over with his junior assistant from the Boston Navy Yard in his car, which was waiting at the door. They went, accordingly, and before they reached the half-way mark, the skies cleared, the sun came out, shining bright and warm. Mr. Hill drove rapidly and before the Navy man realized it they had reached Schoodic. Mr. Hill and the junior engineer walked on ahead while Captain Hooper, lame from his exploring trip the day before, declared he would remain behind, but, seeing them disappear, he hobbled after and finally reached the site, finding it pleasant beyond expectation in the October sunshine. He returned and reported on it in an altered mood.

Our difficulties vanished; those at Washington began. The National Park Service, discouraged by the difficulties encountered, had come to look upon the project for the removal of the Radio Station to another site as dead. And now, with no funds reserved, it was faced with the necessity of building a road some miles in length and adequate to the new radio station's need without means to build it.

A last minute attempt was made to get the Navy Department to reconsider a site which had been earlier proposed and rejected near the coast guard station on Little Cranberry Island, off the Northeast Harbor shore, where no new road construction would be called for, but against this as an island site, the Navy Department remained adamant.

Finally funds were scraped together to build a less ambitious road, further from the shore and narrower than regulation width, which might serve for present needs. Nevertheless the road was beautiful and the contract let was faithfully carried out, though the construction to my regret was made at a loss to the contractor.

Once the way had been cleared for the transfer of the Naval Radio Station to Schoodic, an appropriation for a building became immediately necessary. The best that could be built was virtually pledged to the Navy in exchange for its consent to move. Navy Department engineers submitted an estimate which called for $350,000. This I believed to be needlessly high, and, obtaining an itemized statement from them, cut off $100,000, leaving $250,000 to be obtained. This I assured the Director, Mr. Albright, would be sufficient.

So for this we asked, going together to the Director of the Budget to get it entered. We found him, with two colleagues, at his office. The budget estimates for the coming year had just been sent across to President Hoover but there was still time, they thought, to get our item entered. Director Albright returned to his office; I stayed on. The Director of the Budget, becoming interested, offered to take our item over to the President that afternoon and explain it to him — there was no time to lose. This he did; the item was entered and the appropriation passed. Another day and we should have been too late.

Later that summer, the full scope and seriousness of the financial depression for the first time realized, a cut of ten per cent on all appropriations was passed by Congress and approved by the President. Our building fund, for whose sufficiency I had made myself responsible to the Director, shrank correspondingly. But what remained was still sufficient for an adequate and spacious building.

Urge the plans forward as best I could, however, they were still far from completed when the new administration under President Roosevelt came in and all appropriations not secured by contract were impounded, those for our Naval Radio Station building among the rest. The new Director of the Budget, Lewis Douglas, was firm in making no releases save those the need for which stood on the most solid ground. Our one chance was to persuade him that ours stood on that basis. It was accomplished, not without difficulty, and plans were rushed that the contract might be let before our construction fund should lapse with the conclusion of the Government's fiscal year, July first. In this we succeeded and the work commenced. In February, 1935, the building was completed and the transfer of the Naval Radio Station from Otter Cliffs to Schoodic was carried out.

To me the radio is a constant wonder and its presence at Schoodic, guiding ships at sea from that hitherto so wild and lonely point and receiving communications from far distant ports, is a miracle beyond belief.

Agreement reached for the removal of the Otter Cliffs Radio Station to its new site, Mr. Rockefeller, the conditions he had laid down fulfilled, continued his reconstruction of the Ocean Drive and began work on its continuation around Otter Cliffs Point, adding to it a unique, magnificent feature, terminating his work ultimately in a round turn and parking ground opposite the former Radio Station site.

While I was in Washington during the spring of 1933, urging on, till safe-guarded by contract let, the plans for our new Schoodic Radio Station, and the nation-wide depression was plunging down into new depths, two measures, springing from it, were adopted by the Government whose importance to the Park it would be difficult to over-estimate.

The establishment of Civilian Conservation Corps Camps, the C. C. C., in aid of youth and the combatting of unemployment; and the purchase by the Government from impoverished owners of economically unprofitable lands.

Under the first I made application for two camps for Acadia National Park, the one upon the eastern, the other on the western side of the Island. Under the land purchase measure I marked out upon the map an area of some five thousand acres west of Southwest Harbor, extending from the mountains to the sea, whose central feature was the once drained and cultivated but now reverted to the wild Bass Harbor marshes, an ideal breeding ground and sanctuary for aquatic birds, lying directly under the ancient and still travelled Atlantic coast migration route of which such wonderful accounts have come down to us from early travellers and explorers.

The two camps were granted and have furnished the Park with all the labor which it has had, road construction apart, since their establishment and have enabled it to carry on, uninterruptedly, important work.

The land acquisition measure, more doubtful of execution at the start, lay in the doldrums until the fall but then took on new life. Learning this, I telegraphed at once to Assistant Director Wirth, in charge of this for the National Park Service, to whose friendly interest, on leaving Washington. I had entrusted the map on which I had outlined in broad red pencil the areas I was anxious to secure. Action quickly followed, its first stage the dispatching of a man from Washington to look our proposition over; the second, the plan approved, the appointment of an agent, Mr. Schuyler R. Clark of Southwest Harbor, to undertake the securing of options — a work requiring endless patience and familiarity with the local situation.

To him the Government added, soon after, as Land Appraiser, Mr. Clarence E. Dow, intimately conversant likewise with the people of the Island's western side, their ownerships, their characters and needs. Working together for the next two years, they accomplished results beyond expectation, securing practically all I had asked for and important tracts besides.

But this was not all, for, the depression continuing and men thrown widely out of work the country over, the Government established agencies where the need was greatest to provide employment at the Federal expense, on work, if possible, of permanent importance. This led to the employment under Mr. Dow's direction of a considerable force on the development of the Government's newly acquired parklands, thus securing not the lands only but their development as well, leaving them transformed from waste and desolate areas into recreationally valuable parklands and wild life preserves.

OLDFARM, GEORGE DORR'S HOME

A FORWARD GLANCE

The Gift of Oldfarm

The first announcement of the outbreak of the second World War was made by the Associated Press on September first, 1939, in their news dispatch:

"Hitler Bombs Warsaw!"

We all, in America no less than England, recognized at once the fateful implication of that statement and the demand it made on all of us for co-operation to the full.

Deeply stirred by the daily news that came to us of the progress of the war as it swept over France and the Low Countries and invaded England, desperately resisting, I wrote the President on August first, 1940, the following letter:

Dear President Roosevelt:

Though we are not as yet ourselves involved in what is happening abroad, I know the grave concern which it must give you and the need of some quiet place through the coming weeks where you can think undisturbed and consult with your councillors; and I write to offer you in free gift my old family home, Oldfarm, on the shore of Frenchmans Bay, knowing no other contribution I can make so valuable as to give you the rest and quiet you need for the remainder of the summer, that you may return to Washington in the fall with renewed strength and vigor.

The grounds about Oldfarm are spacious, connecting directly with lands of Acadia National Park, into whose origin they entered largely some years since. All these grounds may be subject to the most strict control to protect you from interruption, while on the other side Oldfarm borders directly upon the sea with a well-protected harbor all its own.

Hoping that my offer and its purpose may appeal to you, believe me to remain, with ever high regard.

Sincerely yours,

George Bucknam Dorr

To this the President replied, thanking me for my offer but saying that he knew of no way by which the President personally could accept such a gift. He added, however, that the end I sought could, if I saw fit, be accomplished by offering it to the Government through the Secretary of the Interior, already empowered by Act of Congress to accept whatever gift might be offered the nation for the benefit and greater usefulness of Acadia National Park.

This, which was in direct line with the thought I already had in my mind concerning the future of the estate, carried a strong appeal to me and, after a full study of what this step, if taken, should carry with it, I set things in order without delay for carrying out the suggestion.

The first step I realized as essential in establishing this closer tie between our old homestead on the shore, with all its memories and associations, and the National Park office site and buildings was to make the latter permanent and secure by changing the status upon which they were used by the Government from that of rental from the Wild Gardens of Acadia to that of ownership. This, involving a financial transaction, required an Act of Congress and for it, unable at that time to go to Washington myself, I turned to my old friend, Edward T. Taylor of Colorado, the oldest in service and best beloved member of the House of Representatives, who promptly, on my getting in touch with him, introduced the bill and placed himself behind it. To this I added what had been suggested by the President's reply and I had already had in mind myself in looking forward to the future, the gift of Oldfarm itself to the National Park Service, bringing the Park down in permanent ownership to contact with the sea on a beautiful and well-harbored coast.

The Bill, carried out in full accordance with Congressman Taylor's advice, passed just before the close of the Congressional session of 1941. Shortly after this Congressman Taylor died. Had the matter come up later, I could not have had the benefit of his friendly interest and long experience in Washington.

Only a few weeks after the Bill had been finally approved and details alone remained to carry out, came the attack of the Japanese on our fleet at Pearl Harbor which brought us unitedly, at a single stroke, into the war ourselves. After that, nothing relating to other than wartime matters could have gained attention from either the President or Congress.

The war is still continuing, the outlines of its future still uncertain; but there is nothing in my work for the Island or the Park that I look back upon with greater satisfaction or sense of permanence.

EPILOGUE

Acadia National Park has experienced many changes since the passing of George Dorr. It has grown to more than 40,000 acres, encompasses several islands in addition to its holdings on Mount Desert and the mainland, has established "fixed" boundaries, offers a wide array of naturalist programs to millions of summer visitors each year, and has become a shining jewel in the crown of the National Park System.

There have been periods of controversy and times of concern, however. Today, the concerns are with the overuse of the Park's most scenic overlooks, the deterioration of the trails and paths, and the constant need for more money to maintain what Dorr and his successors established. In his day there were 50 plus miles of groomed carriage roads, 250 miles of cut and cleared trails, and far fewer people attempting to use the roads and byways of Acadia.

This summer's visitors will have far fewer miles of hiking and walking trails, and those which exist will not be maintained to the levels experienced by the "rusticators." Organizations such as the Friends of Acadia have been working to acquire funds for path restoration. In addition, there are now volunteer groups who work on a weekly basis during the summer to retrieve some of the 150 miles of paths which are slowly being lost.

Many of the goals and dreams of President Eliot, George Dorr, and John Rockefeller remain to be realized, but they would be proud of today's Park. We owe a great debt to them, and to those men and women who followed them.

Remember, this magnificent park is ours! We can each make a contribution to its future by donating money or time, by volunteering for path restoration, by not leaving trash behind, by respecting the flora and fauna of this wonderland, and — most importantly — by enjoying it to the fullest, at every opportunity.